Increase Your Score in
3 MINUTES a Day

ACT
Reading

Also in this series

Increase Your Score in 3 Minutes a Day: ACT Essay,
McCutcheon and Schaffer

Increase Your Score in 3 Minutes a Day: SAT Critical Reading,
McCutcheon and Schaffer

Increase Your Score in 3 Minutes a Day: SAT Essay,
McCutcheon and Schaffer

Increase Your Score in
3 MINUTES a Day
ACT
Reading

RANDALL MCCUTCHEON AND JAMES SCHAFFER, PH.D.

New York   Chicago   San Francisco   Lisbon   London   Madrid   Mexico City
Milan   New Delhi   San Juan   Seoul   Singapore   Sydney   Toronto

Library of Congress Cataloging-in-Publication Data

McCutcheon, Randall, 1949–
    Increase your score in 3 minutes a day. ACT reading / Randall McCutcheon,
James Schaffer.
        p.   cm.
    Includes bibliographical references (p. 136).
    ISBN 0-07-145667-8
        1. ACT Assessment—STUDY guides.   2. Reading comprehension—
Examinations—Study guides.   I. Title: Increase your score in three minutes a
day. ACT reading.   II. Title: ACT reading.   III. Schaffer, James, 1949–.
IV. Title.

LB2353.48.M34   2005
378.1′662—dc22   2005043762

10 11 12 13 14 DOC/DOC 1 5 4 3 2 1 0

ISBN 978-0-07-145667-8
MHID   0-07-145667-8

Interior design by Cheryl McLean
Interior illustrations:
Pages xiv and 62 © Sidney Harris. Reprinted with permission.
Pages 7 and 41 © 2003 Hilary B. Price. Reprinted with special permission of King Features
    Syndicate.
Pages 22 and 36 © 2003 ZITS Partnership. Reprinted with special permission of King
    Features Syndicate.
Page 27 © 1997 ZITS Partnership. Reprinted with special permission of King Features
    Syndicate.
Page 46 Calvin and Hobbes © 1990 Watterson. Reprinted by permission of Universal
    Press Syndicate. All rights reserved.
Page 69 © The New Yorker Collection 1996 Tom Cheney from cartoonbank.com. All rights
    reserved.
Page 86 by David Ernest Lyon

Contents

Preface

I f you pick up a paper only to glance at the comics, chances are that you are more smart aleck than smart. But you are not alone. Researcher William Albert says, "You can walk through whole neighborhoods of houses in this country that do not contain books or magazines—unless you count catalogs."

More and more people who can read, don't. These people who don't read are known as aliterates. In the *Washington Post* article "The No-Book: Skim It and Weep," aliteracy is described as "an invisible liquid, seeping through our culture, nigh on impossible to pinpoint or defend against."

So how pervasive is aliteracy? Kylene Beers, a professor of reading at the University of Houston, says, "About 100 percent of first-graders walk in on the first day and are interested in this thing called reading. Eighty percent of graduating seniors tell us they will never voluntarily pick up a book again."

Big mistake. You need to read as much as possible. It's not about time. It's about choices. Do you check out what's happening at the mall or check out a book? Play Sim City or read *A Tale of Two Cities*? You must decide each time.

Your first good choice today is to read this book. If you follow the advice contained in these pages, you will increase your score on the Reading section of the ACT. But there is a greater purpose here. This book will help you rediscover the joy of reading. And that, dear reader, is no laughing matter.

—Randall J. McCutcheon

Acknowledgments

The authors would like to thank the following:

Jane Durso
David Lyon
Dee Schaffer
Tom Schaffer
Antonia Welsh

Introduction

From the Greek philosophy of a filled storehouse to the statue in the film *Animal House*, we have been reminded that "Knowledge Is Good." Consider this sage advice in Al Franken's book *Oh, the Things I Know!*:

> *It doesn't matter what you learn, just that you remain committed to learning. Make a solemn pledge to learn at least one new thing a week. This week I'm learning the names of the Great Lakes. Next week I'm learning Italian. But that's next week.*

Then again, maybe you don't have time to learn Italian next week. Or much else. This book offers you an efficient way to master reading skills. *Pronto.*

Please note that the following kinds of questions may be asked about the Reading passages:

- **Vocabulary in Context questions.** By studying words in context, you must be able to determine their meanings.
- **Literal Comprehension questions.** Your understanding of specific information directly stated in the passage will be assessed.
- **Extended Reading questions.** These questions are the most challenging. Information must be analyzed and synthesized. You may be asked to evaluate the assumptions of an author. You should know how to identify cause and effect, make inferences, recognize implications, and follow the logic of an argument.

Simple enough, you say. Unfortunately, more than 600,000 of the freshmen entering college in a recent year enrolled in a remedial reading, writing, or math class. That would be about 29 percent of the entire freshman class. Evidently, being able to read is not a prerequisite for college admission. Education reporter John Cloud asks the obvious question: "Should you be allowed into college if you don't read well enough to understand your local paper?"

Comedian Dave Chappelle might respond: "A jump shot is a terrible thing to waste." Of course, life might not have been a slam dunk for you. Coach may never have sent you into the game. What then? Casey McCall, a character on the television show "Sports Night," once explained Napoleon's strategy at Waterloo. According to McCall, Napoleon had a two-part plan. The first part: "Just show up." The second part: "See what happens." There is a lesson for you here. If you follow Napoleon's strategy in preparing for the Reading passages, you will likely suffer the same defeat.

This book offers a plan that works. And you won't have to skip to your Waterloo.

"CAN'T YOU GUYS READ?"

Making This Book Work for You

··

I f you're a high school student on the go (and what high school student isn't?), you could download some new software on your cell phone. The software offers about six hundred practice questions and test-taking strategies for the ACT. In a gamelike feature, users can compete against a clock, against other players, or even across the Internet.

A better bet (and a cheaper one) is to make the most of this book. In the next few pages you'll learn about several different approaches—ways to get the most out of your studying, depending on how much time you have before the test.

In the meantime, however, be sure to consider the single best plan for doing well on the ACT—take tough classes. As Richard Ferguson, ACT's CEO, puts it, "Not only is the number of courses important, but the quality and intensity of these classes will determine if a high school student is ready for college and work." So tough it out.

By the way, ACT no longer stands for American College Testing, though it once did. As the company expanded its programs to include work skills tests and professional certification, it changed its name: ACT is no longer an acronym (a bunch of letters that stand for a series of words); it's just the company's name.

The Basic Approach

The Seven-Week, 3-Minutes-a-Day Plan

Day 1: Study the Introduction and Making This Book Work for You sections.

Days 2–16: Study one Principle each day. Then, three times throughout the day, review in your head the essential ideas taught in that day's principle. The next morning in the shower say aloud those same essential ideas. Repeat. And not just the shampoo. Lather, too.

Days 17–26: Begin mastering the Strategies. Use the same daily routine that you learned with the Principles. One Strategy each day.

Days 27–34: Read and answer the questions for one Practice Passage a day. Review the Principles and Strategies that apply to the questions.

Days 35–44: Review the Strategies one more time.

Day 45: Celebrate. Take as long as you like.

The Last-Minute Approach ... or ACT-CPR

You've procrastinated. The ACT is only a week away. How do you resuscitate your chances for Reading success? Our prescription: choose one of the following two protocols.

Protocol 1: Skip the Principles sections. For three days, spend the minutes you've allocated for study to the Strategies. Do five of the passages each day over the next three days. On the seventh day, rest and review.

Protocol 2: This protocol requires additional time each day but is a more thorough "treatment." Thus, the prognosis for recovery is better. On the first three days, study the Principles section. Work on the Practice Passages for the next three days. On the seventh day, rest and review.

What is that word that a doctor shouts when an emergency-room patient goes into cardiac arrest? Oh yeah, "Clear."

CLEAR!

Good news. You have a pulse. So defibril . . . later. Study now.

PRINCIPLES
OF READING

* *

There is something in the American character that is
secretly hostile to the act of aimless reading.
  —Anna Quindlen

America values sociability and community, notes novelist and former *New York Times* columnist Anna Quindlen, and unfortunately too often associates "nose in the book" readers with loners and losers. But learning to read well is as vital to your success as it has been to Quindlen's, in college and beyond.

In the following pages you will find fifteen reading principles that are tried-and-true techniques. They will help you increase your reading speed, know what to read and what to skip, learn how to mark up a passage to make review easy, quickly identify the thesis and supporting points, summarize what you've read to help find answers, discover what words mean from their contexts, and much more.

The only losers in the ACT game are those who can't read. So buck up your courage and prepare to become a topflight reader.

Rev That Engine, Parnelli!

Good readers have the mind-set of a race-car driver. They press the pedal to the metal on the straightaways and slow down on the curves. In other words, they vary their reading speed depending on what they want to accomplish. You should too.

The passages in the ACT Reading test are about 750 words. Your aim should be to spend no more than about three to four minutes reading each passage. To do so, you should try to average at least 200 words per minute. That will leave you about forty seconds to answer each question.

The average college student reads between 250 and 350 words per minute on fiction and nontechnical material. Some people can read a thousand words per minute or even faster, but the ACT isn't about speed-reading—it's about reading for meaning.

Nevertheless, research has shown that the faster you read, the more likely you are to remember what you've read. Slow reading—plodding along word by word—inhibits understanding. With a little guided practice, most people can double their reading speed without lowering their comprehension.

Here are some techniques that may help you increase how fast you read:

1. **Avoid regressing** (going back over what you've already read). Rereading words and phrases is a habit that will slow your reading down to a snail's pace. Usually, it is unnecessary to reread words, as the ideas you want are explained and elaborated more fully later in the passage.

If you read slowly, your mind has time to wander. Even worse, if you find yourself doing so, this reflects both an inability to concentrate and a lack of confidence in your comprehension skills (think of the student who never hears the directions the first time).

2. **Develop a wider eye span.** This will help you read more than one word at a glance. Since written material is less meaningful if read word by word, this will help you learn to read by phrases or thought units.

3. **Learn to adjust your rate to your purpose in reading and to the difficulty of the material.** The effective reader adjusts his or her rate; the ineffective reader uses the same rate for all types of material.

   Suppose you took a 100-mile mountain trip by car. You might plan to average about fifty miles an hour, but in reality, you slow down to twenty on some hills and curves and speed up to seventy on certain straightaways. The same concept holds true with reading.

   In general, slow down when you find the following:

   • unfamiliar terms not immediately clear from context
   • difficult sentence or paragraph structure
   • abstract concepts
   • detailed technical material (complicated directions, for example)

   On the other hand, increase your reading speed when you encounter:

   • simple material with few ideas that are new to you
   • unnecessary examples or illustrations
   • broad, general ideas or ideas that are restatements of previous ones

Keep your reading attack flexible; adjust your rate from passage to passage and within each passage. The crucial skill is to be able to change speed, to know when to slow down or speed up.

Pacing is particularly important on the Reading passages—if you spend too much time reading the passages, you won't leave enough time for the questions. Don't sweat the details. Don't waste time reading and rereading parts you don't understand. Make sure you leave time for answering the questions, which is what really counts.

Know When
and What to Skip

What you bring to your reading is far more important than the words themselves. All the knowledge you've gained from life so far—both the knowledge of the world and the knowledge of how written works are constructed—helps you know what a passage means. In a strange sense, you know what you're going to read before you even start.

Let's take a closer look at that apparent paradox. The secret of reading efficiently is to sample the text and make predictions. The reader takes chances and risks making errors, in order to predict what a passage means. Unless the reader feels free to take chances and make mistakes, he or she can never make any real headway.

We read to identify meaning, not to identify letters or words. A reader cannot process letters, words, and meanings all at the same time. Natural limitations in our memory systems prevent it (for example, we can remember phone numbers, but just barely—seven digits is about our max). We slow down to look at letters, letter clusters, or words only when we are surprised or confused—when what we expected to read wasn't there.

The reader guesses the meaning of unfamiliar words from context or else just skips them. Even in textbook or technical material, the best strategy is to skip a new word the first time it appears, expecting it to be explained or defined contextually before too long. Of course, if the new word is not explained, keeps reappearing, and seems to be important, then the reader can use a dictionary or guess. But consider if you are engrossed in a personal letter from a friend or an exciting novel. Do you stop when you read an unfamiliar word? Of course not.

As a good reader, you take an active role, bringing to bear your knowledge of the world and of the particular topic in the passage. You read as though you expect the passage to make sense. Therefore, with difficult or unfamiliar material, the best approach may be to push ahead, especially on the first reading, trusting that the reading will become easier as you continue predicting meaning, making guesses, and taking chances.

If you didn't do these things, psycholinguists tell us, you couldn't read at all. Their research suggests that the reader relies as little as possible on visual information. Good readers sample the passage economically, searching for major points and key terms.

What happens when your predictions go awry (as they will, from time to time)? You correct surprises by circling back when tentative interpretations or predictions are not successful. At the same time, however, you maintain enough speed to overcome the limitations of the visual processing and memory systems.

Crystal Ball Grazing

L ook deeply into this crystal ball. Can you see your future? Yes, the one where your house is featured on MTV's "Cribs" and you've just been signed to a multimillion-dollar contract to promote a new soft drink.

Predicting the future isn't just for soothsayers and television prophets. Readers, too, proceed by making predictions about the passage. We are rarely aware that we are making predictions for the simple reason that our predictions are usually so good. Our predictions rarely let us down, even when we read a book for the first time.

What exactly do we predict when we read? The fundamental answer is meaning. Prediction is the reason that the brain is not overwhelmed by all the possible alternatives in a passage; for example, if you reach the bottom of a page and see this sentence: "The captain told the crew to drop an-", you don't really need to turn the page to know that an "anchor" is just about to plop into the sea. We expect what the writer is likely to say because consciously or not, we are continually making predictions about the text.

Let's look at how this might work in the ACT Reading exam. Suppose you find a passage that begins like this:

> *One evening in late January, Peter Dut, twenty-one, leads his two teenage brothers through the brightly lit corridors of the Minneapolis airport, trying to mask his confusion.*

We immediately grasp the basic situation: we have a narrative involving several characters (Peter and his two brothers), a setting (January in Minneapolis, brrrr!), and a conflict (Peter is confused).

What we're not told—why Peter is in Minneapolis in the first place and why he's so confused—helps stimulate our desire to predict. We expect to find answers to those questions as the passage continues, and by predicting what those answers will be we become more active readers. Here's the next sentence:

> *Two days earlier, the brothers, refugees from Africa,*
> *encountered their first light switch and their first set of stairs.*

Part of the mystery is solved. We know the boys are from Africa, and from a very undeveloped part, apparently. But part of the mystery remains open: how is it that they have come to Minneapolis? This process will be repeated over and over again as we read. We will find a few answers that in turn lead to more questions.

Let's see what happens next:

> *An aid worker in Nairobi demonstrated the flush toilet to*
> *them—also the seat belt, the shoelace, the fork. And now they*
> *find themselves alone in Minneapolis, three bone-thin African*
> *boys confronted by a swirling river of white faces and rolling*
> *suitcases.*

Images from Africa (the "river of white faces") blend in the boys' imaginations with new sensations ("rolling suitcases") to create a cultural jumble. Now we can predict what the narrative is heading toward: a series of cultural encounters between these African boys and American technology. And indeed, as we read in the article "The Lost Boys" by Sara Corbett, we learn the story of some 3,600 Sudanese refugees who have come to the United States to find new lives.

Pay special attention to first and last words of a paragraph—do they remind you of something you read in the previous paragraph or help prepare you for the succeeding one? Look for parallels in content and style. Often writers will emphasize a point by repeating the structure of a particular sentence or repeating a particularly significant word.

As you read the ACT passages, keep asking yourself: Where is this headed? What can I expect to find? Making guesses and predictions will keep you alert and engaged as a reader. It puts you in control.

Finally, polish up that mental crystal ball you've been saving for just this occasion.

Writing Between the Lines

You ought to hold something in your hand while you read. No, not a glass of iced tea. Not even a Snickers, though that's not a bad idea. What we're talking about is a pencil.

The pencil represents your alertness. It acts as a symbol of the active reader. Use the pencil as you read to mark the passage.

Students are sometimes reluctant to write on a book. If the book belongs to the school, that's a good policy. But if the book belongs to you, make it your own and mark all over it. That's the real way to claim it as your property.

In the case of the ACT test, you're free to mark up the reading passages. Don't miss this opportunity. Marking the passage accomplishes two very important goals:

1. It keeps you alert. With that pencil in hand, you have the sense that you're doing something as you read, not simply absorbing information passively.
2. It makes it easy to review. When you go back over a passage, you can quickly return to key points and terms that you've already identified.

Here are a couple of techniques to help you mark a passage effectively and efficiently:

- Underline key points or ideas.
- Use vertical lines in the margins when the section you want to highlight is too long to underline.

- Use stars or asterisks to indicate the thesis statement of a passage.
- Use numbers to indicate key supporting details.
- Circle key words or terms. These can be terms that seem especially important or, occasionally, terms that seem to be used in a strange or unusual way.
- Write in the margins or at the top or bottom of the page. These are the places to jot down a few thoughts. Make note of any questions you might have. In the case of the ACT, if you have looked ahead at the questions, write down possible answers—before you look at the answers the test makers offer.

Keeping a pencil handy as you read makes reading a more active, physical process. If you can do something to keep your body (as well as your mind) in motion, you have a much better chance of understanding and remembering what you read (see Strategy 5 for additional ideas).

X-Ray Vision

Remember the Terminator? In those movies, the main character is a robot that looks human. In other words, beneath his flesh and blood lies a metal skeleton (never mind that the actor who played him, Arnold Schwarzenegger, was better at playing robots than humans).

An x-ray would have quickly revealed the Terminator's identity. Using x-ray vision (metaphorically speaking), you can also quickly discover the skeleton, or structure, beneath the surface of the words in a passage. The surface features, whether of text or robot, can be deceiving, but if you can discern what lies beneath, you will have a true sense of the passage's meaning.

You can learn to use x-ray vision to help you answer three questions about any given chunk of prose:

1. **What is the passage about?** By quickly scanning the entire passage, you can grasp a sense of the writer's topic and probably something about the writer's approach.

   Is the work mainly fact or fiction? Is the work from the world of science (you'll be tipped off, most likely, by the presence of technical terms and references to experiments) or social sciences (trends, correlations, causes, and consequences)? Is the text written in first person or third person? The answers to these questions help set the stage for this one:

2. **What are the parts or sections of the passage?** If the writer is worth her salt, she will have presented some support for her main point. Can you recognize the nature of that support? Typically, an author will present several reasons or examples

to convince the reader that the thesis is true. If you can recognize these subpoints, you will be able to see the passage fall neatly into sections.

Most passages can be organized into a hierarchy with the thesis on top, supporting points below, and explanatory details even farther down. Once you see the pattern, you can zero in on what you really want to know or what question you're trying to answer. Finally, use your x-ray vision to answer this last question:

3. **How do the parts fit together?** Each passage may have a beginning, middle, and end, but not necessarily in that order. So pay attention to transition words and terms. Some transition words tell you that the writer is continuing a particular chain of thought by adding information. These words and phrases include: *additionally, also, moreover, not only, but, another, furthermore,* and *for example.* Other transition words and phrases may signal a change or reversal: *however, on the other hand, but,* and *yet.* Still others tell you the writer is reaching a conclusion: *therefore, then, thus, in sum,* and *in short.*

If you have a clear idea of the overall development of the passage, you will be able to answer thesis questions more easily and understand how the various parts of the argument fit together. Be on the lookout for contrasting points of view. Most selections will present one argument and briefly describe a competing or conflicting idea. Fictional passages may pit what the main character thinks against what others think.

It may also be true that your x-ray vision will spot a broken bone, in other words, a flaw, in the passage. Perhaps one of the subpoints is not fully developed, or maybe the thesis comes after some of the supporting information. In any event, learning to develop x-ray vision will reveal to you whatever lurks beneath the surface.

Something Worth Arguing About

The typical ACT reading passage will contain a thesis statement, usually in the first paragraph. The thesis statement will let the reader know, as soon as possible, what argument the passage will make. Identifying this thesis statement is the most important reading task you have.

A thesis is the largest, broadest statement in the passage. It should have these three characteristics:

1. It is something worth arguing about. There is no point in basing a passage on a thesis that is obvious to everyone or that isn't concerned with a significant issue. Read the statement you identify as the thesis, and ask yourself, "So what?" If you can't answer that question, you probably haven't found the true thesis.
2. It is precise. It is not something anyone has trouble understanding and is not so general that it fails to represent a strong position.
3. It is supported by the rest of the passage; it isn't just a springboard that allows the writer to jump into topics having little to do with the thesis.

Let's try that test on the following passage, taken from a *Smithsonian* article by Andrew Curry on the first human flight, that of the Wright brothers at Kitty Hawk in 1903:

As an Air Force test pilot, Lt. Col. Dawn Dunlop has flown dozens of different airplanes, from the nimble F-I SE Strike Eagle fighter to the massive C-17 transport jet to the Russian MIG-21. Stationed at Edwards Air Force Base, she's part of the elite squadron that is putting the cutting-edge F/A-22 Raptor, a jet fighter, through its paces. But the aircraft that Dunlop has had the toughest time controlling was a replica of the Wright brothers' glider. More than once she crash-landed the muslin-skinned craft on to the windswept sands of Kitty Hawk, North Carolina. "It was a real eye-opener," Dunlop recalls of the (bruising) experience last year, part of a commemorative Air Force program. "They've made it so simple to fly today we've forgotten how difficult it was back then."

In this passage, the writer introduces us to an Air Force test pilot, someone who has flown the world's most advanced and sophisticated aircraft. And yet, it turns out, the toughest plane she ever flew was a replica of the Wright brothers' glider. That background, which provides a useful context for the reader, prepares us for the thesis statement—the last sentence in the paragraph. We could paraphrase it like this: "Flying seems simple today, so simple we have forgotten how difficult it was in the beginning of human flight." Does that sentence meet our test?

1. **Is it worth arguing about?** Certainly. The magazine's blurb reinforces the thesis this way: "From the Wright brothers' breakthrough 100 years ago to the latest robot jets, the past century has been shaped by the men and women who got us off the ground." Reviewing the story of the Wright brothers will help us put modern aviation progress in perspective.

2. **Is it precise?** "Back then" in the thesis refers specifically to the Wright brothers and their famous flight in December 1903.

3. **Is it supported by the passage?** Some of the references in the passage to modern aircraft seem at first glance to be off target. But on further reflection, it's clear that they provide a useful contrast to the simplicity of that first flight.

Here's one final test: a good thesis answers a question. What that question is, however, is something you'll have to figure out. In this case, the question might be: why is the Wright brothers' flight significant today? If the thesis statement you've identified in an ACT passage can be viewed as an answer to a question the writer wanted to ask, you have probably zeroed in on just the right sentence.

Summarily Dismissed

E very passage you read will present a different challenge, but being able to summarize what you read will help you become a more active reader, someone who can quickly grasp what he's reading. As you'll discover, being able to say in a few words what has taken someone else a great many can be difficult. But like any other skill, the ability to summarize improves with practice.

Here are a few pointers to get you started. Be prepared, however, to vary your technique to fit the situation.

1. **As you read, pay close attention to the author's purpose.** This will help you distinguish between more important and less important information.

2. **Write a one-sentence summary of the entire passage.** Consider what a newspaper reporter would want to know: the who, what, why, where, when, and how. The idea of a summary is to clarify and condense. Your goal is to create a miniature version of the passage, to repeat its essence but telescoped in size and scale. Summarize the author's ideas in the order in which he has presented them, but avoid following his wording too closely.

3. **Check your summary against the original passage.** Make whatever adjustments are necessary for accuracy and completeness. Notice what you've left out. Is it essential or can it be safely disregarded?

For practice, take a look at the following passage from Jon Krakauer's thrilling book about mountain climbing, *Into Thin Air*:

> *People who don't climb mountains—the great majority of humankind, that is to say—tend to assume that the sport is a reckless, Dionysian pursuit of ever escalating thrills. But the notion that climbers are merely adrenaline junkies chasing a righteous fix is a fallacy, at least in the case of Everest. What I was doing up there had almost nothing in common with bungee jumping or skydiving or riding a motorcycle at 120 miles per hour.*
>
> *Above the comforts of Base Camp, the expedition in fact became an almost Calvinistic undertaking. The ratio of misery to pleasure was greater by an order of magnitude than any other mountain I'd been on; I quickly came to understand that climbing Everest was primarily about enduring pain. And in subjecting ourselves to week after week of toil, tedium, and suffering, it struck me that most of us were probably seeking, above all else, something like a state of grace.*

The most important thing the author tries to do in this passage is to correct a common assumption, namely that mountain climbers do it for thrills. Instead, he argues, climbers endure the work, boredom, and suffering that a climb entails to achieve a state of mind, or a serenity of soul, if you will. A summary statement to that effect might look like this:

> *Contrary to popular opinion, people who climb extreme peaks are seeking food for the soul, not thrills for the gut.*

When you are summarizing, review any sentences you have underlined or highlighted to be sure you haven't left anything out. The main difficulty is to determine what is important and what is not. Some parts of the passage—the introduction, examples, and anecdotes—can probably be ignored. Others, including the author's purpose, theme, and key words, must not be.

Be Chalant

*It had been a rough day, so when I walked into
the party I was very chalant, despite my efforts to appear
gruntled and consolate.
I was furling my wieldy umbrella for the coat check when I saw
her standing alone in a corner. She was a descript person, a
woman in a state of total array. Her hair was kempt, her
clothing sheveled, and she moved in a gainly way.*

—Jack Winter

Notice anything missing in that passage? How about a few crucial prefixes—those little syllables that appear at the beginnings of words and provide important ingredients of meaning. (For the record, substitute these words in the passage above and see if things make more sense: *nonchalant, disgruntled, disconsolate, unfurling, unwieldy, nondescript, disarray, unkempt, disheveled,* and *ungainly.*)

Words are not merely groups of letters aimlessly thrown together. They are composed of meaningful elements so arranged as to give each its own significance. For example, many words can be divided into beginnings, middles, and ends. The beginning is a prefix, the middle is the root, and the ending is the suffix.

One of the most economical ways of expanding your vocabulary is to become familiar with the most common affixes (prefixes and suffixes). In doing so, you will acquire clues to the meanings of thousands of words. Furthermore, you will find that spelling becomes easier, for you will see words in their meaningful parts rather than as mere jumbles of letters.

For example, the following English prefixes should already be quite familiar:

after- (later than) as in *afternoon, afterward,* and *afterthought*
fore- (before) as in *forehead, foreword,* and *forecast*
mis- (bad or wrong) as in *misbehavior, misfortune,* and *misfit*

Prefixes often give a negative spin to words. Notice how a prefix turns *stable* into *unstable, mature* into *immature, adequate* into *inadequate,* and *social* into *antisocial.* Some prefixes, on the other hand, suggest relationships: con- (meaning together) gives us *convoy, contain,* and *consent;* circum- (meaning around) yields *circumference, circumspect,* and *circumvent;* inter- (meaning between) provides *intercept, international,* and *interrupt.*

Suffixes (a word's ending syllable or syllables) also play an important part in determining a word's meaning. Notice what a difference the following suffixes make:

employer versus *employee*
thoughtful versus *thoughtless*
waiter versus *waitress*
changeable versus *changeless*

Sometimes you can even combine a prefix and a suffix to make a word. The ending *-cide* (act of killing), for example, can be combined with a variety of prefixes to give us *homicide, suicide,* and *genocide.*

Certainly you can't expect to master every prefix and suffix (though a little practice may pay big dividends). You can use your knowledge of the architecture of words, however—what constitutes their beginning, middle, and end—to make some informed guesses about words you don't know.

Suppose you come across the word *superfluous.* You may be stumped at first, but then you recognize *super-* as a prefix. You know the words *superman* and *superhuman,* so you make a guess that *super* means "over" or "above." Now for the final part of the word: "Hmm, *fluous* sort of looks like *fluid,* so perhaps *superfluous* means 'extra fluid.'" That's not far, by the way, from the dictionary definition—"overflow."

So when you're faced with a difficult word in the ACT exam, divide and conquer. Break the word into its various parts, and see if you can transform several small meanings into one large one.

The Power of Pivot

Imagine a basketball game. The Harlem Globetrotters throw the ball to their center, Meadowlark Lemon. Lemon twists and turns; he takes a step this way, he takes a step that way, but he never moves one foot (his pivot foot)—until he's sure which way he's going. Pivot, the act of turning or changing direction, is a key point in basketball and in writing.

An alert reader will be on the lookout for pivot words and phrases such as *however*, *but*, and *on the other hand*. These words, also called hinge or elbow words, mark a quick turn in the direction the passage is taking from positive to negative, perhaps, or from one point to another.

Let's look at an example. Here is a passage from Joshua P. Warren's book *How to Hunt Ghosts*:

> *Humans have been experiencing things they cannot explain for thousands of years. Most of the world's religions are based on the concept of a spiritual world, or an invisible dimension of existence that transcends our own. However, despite the centuries of "ghostly encounters," such episodes are still considered unexplained.*

Note that pivot word, *however*. Everything in the passage before *however* suggests that humans have long believed in the presence of the supernatural. Everything after *however*, however, suggests that most people don't give any credence to these beliefs. The writer warns the reader with *however* that "that was then, this is now."

Pivot words can sometimes mark a major shift in time, place, or orientation. In this passage from Bill Vaughn's story "Skating Home

Backward," the narrator talks about a childhood dream to ice-skate up the stream beside his house:

> *In the winter, the creek became a different sort of sanctuary. It was a snap to skate the 300 yards from our place to the lagoon where the Missouri accepted the stream, but what I yearned to do was skate to the creek's headwaters, where I would live in tree houses and steal chickens from ranches. It wasn't just the easy pleasure of forward motion that seduced me when I took to the ice, but also the chance to escape all the unpredictable emotional weather back at the house. Yet I never got farther upstream than three miles. When I was old enough to mount a serious quest, it was too late. The creek began running the color of old blood, poisoned by acids and heavy metals leached from the coal mines. The frogs and the fish disappeared first, and finally the turtles. And then it dried up.*

This passage has a small pivot word and another more significant one. The small one is *but*. It highlights the difference between easy tasks (skating 300 yards from home to a nearby lagoon) and difficult ones (skating to the creek's headwaters). The large elbow word is *yet*, not a very impressive looking word, but one that turns the whole passage on its head. Everything before *yet* is youthful, hopeful, and optimistic—about quests and dreams.

What comes after *yet*, however, is dismal—serious adult reality. The creek becomes poisoned by toxic runoff, the frogs and fish die off, and eventually the creek itself disappears. That's a lot of work for a little word like *yet*, and yet, this pivot word is up to the challenge.

Wordlubbers, Beware

As I was going to St. Ives
I met a man with seven wives.
Every wife had seven sacks.
Every sack had seven cats.
Every cat had seven kits.
Kits, cats, sacks, and wives:
How many were going to St. Ives?

If your answer to this riddle is 2,402 (seven times seven times seven times seven plus one), slap yourself silly. You fell for some misdirection. The correct answer, of course, is one—the narrator, or "I," in the poem—who is headed toward St. Ives. All the others he meets must be going in the opposite direction.

This little riddle is a telling example of how nearly all of us can be fooled from time to time by words. By becoming more aware of a few simple language traps, however, you can make yourself much less likely to stumble on the ACT.

Here, for example, is a question that appears to test grammar: Which is correct: "Nine and seven is fifteen" or "Nine and seven are fifteen?" If you said "are," nice going; that's the better of the two answers. But neither answer is correct. Nine and seven are sixteen. (Yes, you're right, we're not supposed to be talking about the math portion of the test right now.) The lesson here is that we often look for the wrong thing because we misunderstand the question. Read difficult questions twice to be sure you know what kind of answer is being sought.

Sometimes we are victims of our own assumptions. Can you solve this puzzle?:

> A doctor is about to operate on a little boy. "This boy is my son," exclaims the doctor. The doctor is correct, yet the doctor isn't the boy's father. What's going on?

This puzzle seems to stump just about everyone, though the answer is really quite simple. The doctor is the boy's mother. Our assumption about doctors—that they're mostly male—is unconscious, but it acts like blinders, keeping us from looking around to find alternative explanations. Be wary of personal prejudices and opinions that may distract you from the real import of a passage.

Here, a different kind of assumption can get in the way:

> Two men play five games of checkers, and each wins the same number of games. There are no ties. How can this be?

If you're stumped, you're in good company. From the way the statement reads, it's easy to assume that the two men have been playing each other. But, in fact, they haven't. The only way they could each win the same number of games is if they were competing against other players. Don't read more into the answer; take it at face value.

Effective reading always requires you to use what you know. Learn to apply the knowledge you've acquired in ten years of school (and more of life). For example, can you figure out this answer?:

> A rope ladder hangs over the side of a ship. The ladder is twelve feet long, and the rungs are one foot apart, with the lowest rung resting on the surface of the ocean. The tide is rising at six inches an hour. How long will it take before the first three rungs of the ladder are underwater?

Landlubbers beware. If you said four hours, you must be from the Midwest. As the tide rises, of course, so do boats. The rung resting on the surface of the ocean will still be there no matter how high or how low the tide might be. As the old saying goes, "A rising tide lifts all boats."

And don't let your boat sink in the ACT exam because of overreading, overinterpreting, unwarranted assumptions, or failure to apply some common sense.

Get a Clue, Holmes

Suppose a stranger were to meet several of your friends before he met you. Would he form an impression of the kind of person you are from the people you spend time with? Probably. Most of us have much in common with the company we keep.

This idea may help you understand how it is possible to learn the meaning of a word without ever looking it up in a dictionary. Good readers, in fact, do this all the time. We say they learn the meaning of a word through its context.

Researchers have shown that most readers could skip every fifth word and still have a good understanding of what they read. Try this sentence from a newspaper, for example:

> *Some working parents wistfully _____ considered keeping their toddlers _____ from day care in _____ hope of isolating them _____ runny noses, coughs, and _____ .*

If your guesses were (in order) *have*, *home*, *the*, *from*, and *germs*, you win the blue ribbon. Even if you only guessed one or two correct answers, you still deduced the words from context.

What this example suggests is that we use the words we recognize in a sentence to help us predict what the other words will be and what they will mean. Pay special attention, for example, to the nonitalicized words in this passage from John McPhee's book on Alaska, *Coming into the Country*:

> *Anchorage has a thin history. Something of a* precursor *of the modern pipeline camps, it began in 1914 as a collection of*

tents pitched to shelter workers building the Alaska Railroad.
For decades, it was a wooden-sidewalked, gravel-streeted
town. Then, remarkably early, as cities go, it developed an
urban slum, and both homes and commerce began to
abandon its core. The exodus *was so rapid that the central*
business district never wholly consolidated, *and downtown*
Anchorage is even more miscellaneous than outlying parts of
the city.

Let's see how other words in the passage can help us discover the meaning of *precursor, exodus,* and *consolidated.* (Pretend for a moment that those words are unfamiliar.)

The first three sentences of the passage contain many references to time—*history, began, 1914, for decades.* This helps us recognize that *precursor* has something to do with time. The prefix, *pre,* is another clue. This prefix should suggest "before" to you (think of *preview, predict,* and *precaution*). Thus, *precursor* must be something that comes before in time; try to think of a synonym—in this case, *predecessor.*

Exodus might be a bit tougher. You know you've heard it before; perhaps you even know it as the name of the second book of the Old Testament. But what the heck does it mean? In the context of this passage, we know that whatever it is, it happens rapidly. It also appears to have something to do with abandon—in the previous sentence we learned that home and business owners have left the city core. The beginning of the word, *ex-,* seems to be a hint (you think of *exit* and *ex-girlfriend,* so it means out or on the outs). Pending further information, which may come later in the passage, you decide *exodus* must mean a hasty departure.

The big clue for the final word, *consolidated,* comes in the form of an antonym or its opposite, in other words. The author of the passage draws a contrast between *consolidated* and *miscellaneous.* Because the city core never consolidated, we are told, it remains miscellaneous. So if we can figure out what *miscellaneous* means, we can be reasonably sure that *consolidated* is just the opposite.

Luckily, you remember that your father had a manila folder labeled "Miscellaneous" lying on the kitchen table the last time he was working on his taxes. He said he threw everything that didn't fit anyplace else in there. If *miscellaneous* means an unorganized mishmash of things, then *consolidated* must mean to unite or combine into a coherent whole. Bingo, you've scored 100 percent on this vocabulary test.

Coming to Terms

Not all words are equal. Or perhaps more accurately, not all words have the same value in a given passage. Inevitably, a writer uses certain words in an especially significant way—either because these words are crucial to the point he or she wants to make or because the author is using a familiar word in a new way. In either case, the writer is turning some words into terms—terms the reader would do well to heed.

We can put it more bluntly: you must spot the important words in a passage and figure out how the author is using them. This challenge has two steps: First, you have to find the important words, the words that make a difference. Second, you have to determine what these words mean as precisely as possible.

So, you ask, how can we tell which of the hundreds of words in a passage are the most important? One way is to notice words that give you trouble. If you notice a word that you don't understand or any word that seems to be used in a peculiar way, you may have located some of the words an author is treating with special significance.

An author may also place explicit stress on certain words. She may, for example, use quotation marks or italics to mark an important word. Notice in the following passage by Dava Sobel how one word appears in italics:

> As a child, I learned the trick for remembering the difference between latitude and longitude. The latitude lines, the *parallels*, really do stay parallel to each other as they girdle the globe from the Equator to the poles in a series of shrinking concentric rings. The meridians of

longitude go the other way: They loop from the North Pole
to the South and back again in great circles of the same
size, so they all converge at the ends of the Earth.

Sobel wants to call the reader's attention to the literal meaning of
parallels as a memory device. Because the reader will read the words
latitude and *longitude* over and over again throughout this book,
the author wants to make a clear and memorable distinction between the two.

Other special words may not be quite as easy to find. Every field
of knowledge has its own special vocabulary. In the Sobel passage
above, we find these words and phrases: *lines, poles, concentric rings,
meridians,* and *converge*—all key terms for mapmakers. Use your
general knowledge to help you. You will certainly recognize some
scientific terms in an article about, say, microorganisms, and the
words you don't recognize are probably scientific terms. You don't
necessarily need to know these terms. It may be enough that you
can recognize them for what they are.

A third way to identify a key term is to notice when the author
makes a fuss. Again in the Sobel passage, she makes a point of
defining meridians for the reader ("They loop from the North Pole
to the South and back again in great circles of the same size"). Here
the writer has anticipated the reader's confusion or, perhaps, lack
of knowledge and dealt with the situation head-on.

In short, the relatively small set of words that express an author's
main ideas make up his special vocabulary. They are the words that
carry his argument. That means these words should be important
for you, too, as a reader. Typically, a number of ACT questions will
ask you about a key term in the passage. We don't want to miss the
forest for the trees, but sometimes it pays to give special attention
to a few key words.

The Harder
It Comes

ome things are hard. Some are harder. When you come to an unusually difficult passage, don't throw up your hands and quit. Regroup.

What makes some Reading passages difficult? You may be given a passage with a particularly obscure topic. The passage may contain abstract ideas or unfamiliar terms. Or you may be intimidated by the subject matter (quantum mechanics, for example, or nuclear fusion). In any of those cases, consider these tactics:

1. **What does the author discuss most?** In this passage from "The Perfect Fire," Sean Flynn describes in colorful detail the various implements a firefighter might carry:

   Every firefighter carries a tool. Some have hoses and ropes, but everyone else wields a piece of medieval hardware—a flat-head ax, for instance, or a Boston Rake, which looks like an old vaudeville hook, except it's made of solid iron and can rip out a plaster ceiling in three swift strokes. Some prefer a Haligan, a rod of hardened steel roughly the size of a baseball bat, with one end flattened into a two-pronged claw. The other end, a flat wedge that can slip between a door and a jamb to pry it open, is attached perpendicularly to the shaft. Next to that, also at a 90-degree angle to the shaft, is an adze, a pear-sized steel point that can puncture the most solid walls and doors.

The odd names of these tools—Boston Rake, Haligan, and adze—may put you off for a moment. "How am I supposed to know what these things are?" you might ask. But don't be discouraged. The author has given us plenty of clues.

For starters, the whole passage is about tools (see sentence #1). You're familiar with tools—they have a design and a function. If you don't completely understand one, you might understand the other. So, for example, the Boston Rake is hard to picture, but it rips out plaster ceilings. What the Haligan does is not entirely clear, but it looks like a baseball bat. By noticing the stress the author places on tools, you can gloss over the details—firefighters have weapons. You don't need much more at this point.

2. **Don't get thrown by the fancy language—just push past it.** Try the following passage. It concerns two of the most important endocrine glands (you know, the ones that regulate our hormones):

> *The hypothalamus regulates the internal environment through the autonomic system. For example, it helps control heartbeat, body temperature, and water balance. The hypothalamus also controls the glandular secretions of the pituitary gland. The pituitary, a small gland about 1 cm in diameter, is connected to the hypothalamus by a stalklike structure. The pituitary has two portions: the anterior pituitary and the posterior pituitary.*

The scientific terms in this passage look as awkward as they are difficult to pronounce. But they need not be insurmountable obstacles. Notice the words and phrases you do recognize—"helps control heartbeat," "a small gland," "connected," and "has two portions." Using these few words alone, you can come up with a reasonable paraphrase of the passage:

"One gland, the hypothalamus, helps control your heartbeat. A small gland, the pituitary, has two parts."

If the question requires you to know more, you can at least begin with this foundation.

3. **Finally, if the passage topic is too difficult to paraphrase, try to answer these essential questions as you read: What is the author's purpose? What is the author's method?** Consider this passage from "Big Money and Politics" by Donald L. Barlett and James B. Steele.

> *It was just your typical piece of congressional dirty work when the House and Senate passed the District of Columbia Appropriations Act. You might think that would be a boring piece of legislation. You would be wrong. For buried in the endless clauses authorizing such spending items as $867 million for education and $5 million to promote the adoption of foster children was Section 6001: Superfund Recycling Equity. It had nothing to do with the District of Columbia, nor appropriations, nor "equity" as it is commonly defined. Instead Section 6001 was inserted in the appropriations bill by Senator Trent Lott of Mississippi, the Senate majority leader, to take the nation's scrap-metal dealers off the hook for millions of dollars in potential Superfund liabilities at toxic-waste sites.*

Anyone could get lost in the numbing numbers and "governmentese" such as *Superfund* and *equity*. But perhaps we can tease out a simple story beneath the obfuscation. The authors' purpose appears to be disabusing us of certain notions or, in other words, revealing to us the true workings of our elected officials. Furthermore, the authors are trying to demonstrate that point by showing us that the title of a piece of legislation (the "Superfund Recycling Equity") is misleading or even false. And voila! If you can reason that far, you probably know all you need to know about that passage.

Difficult? Not on your life.

Reading Fiction

*The Hit Man's early years are complicated by the black bag
that he wears over his head. Teachers correct his pronun-
ciation, the coach criticizes his attitude, the principal dresses
him down for branding preschoolers with a lit cigarette. He is
a poor student. At lunch he sits alone, feeding bell peppers
and salami into the dark slot of his mouth. In the hallways,
wiry young athletes snatch at the black hood and slap the
back of his head. When he is thirteen he is approached by the
captain of the football team, who pins him down and
attempts to remove the hood. The Hit Man wastes him. Five
years, says the judge.*

Welcome to the fun house. If the passage above seems a bit
strange, brace yourself. One-fourth of the passages in the
Reading test are taken from fiction, just like the one above
from a story by T. Coraghessan Boyle. Reading fiction is anything
but straightforward.

The reader uses imagination to enter into the work and remain
absorbed in it. He or she expects to have an aesthetic and emotional
experience. The reader of fiction also assumes that the work has a
unity; that is, everything is interrelated. If a suitcase shows up early
on, you can be sure someone will eventually be taking a trip.

The fictional passages on the ACT exam require a different
approach than the other kinds of passages:

1. **Read for the story, not the structure.** Unlike science passages, fiction doesn't always stick to a rigidly organized struc-

ture. In order to figure out what's going on and answer the questions, you're going to have to concentrate on what's happening among the characters.

For example, in the story "The Hit Man," we meet several characters including the Hit Man himself, a coach, a football captain, and a judge. Clearly, we should focus our attention on the Hit Man—the other characters are only there to help reveal aspects of his nature. And that nature is a bit mysterious. Why does he wear a black bag over his head? Does he think he's Zorro? Is the black bag simply a metaphor? That is, does the Hit Man really wear a bag to school (not likely) or is it an artistic way for the writer to tell us this person keeps his inner feelings hidden?

2. **Read critically.** The ACT questions are going to ask you to go beneath the surface of the narrative, so ask yourself questions as you read. How do the characters feel about each other? What is the narrator's main concern?

In our story the characters only interact to the extent that they oppose or antagonize the Hit Man. What is the author concerned about? Why do others dislike the Hit Man? Why is he so unlikable? Does he resent this treatment? There are no fast and easy answers to these questions, but we're not looking for facts. We're looking instead for puzzles. What issues does the author want us to ponder? What mysteries does he want us to explore?

3. **Note the author's language.** Many of the ACT questions are going to ask you why the author chose certain words or expressions. As you read, keep asking yourself the significance of the language the author uses.

Again, let's look at "The Hit Man." It's noteworthy that none of the characters is given a name. Everyone is identified by his or her role, or at least one narrow aspect of that role— teacher, coach, captain. What might this suggest about the author's approach? That covers the nouns; now what about the verbs? The passage apparently took place years ago and yet is told in present tense. What might this tell us about the author's intent? Is the author reinforcing the idea that whatever happened to the Hit Man in the past is still affecting him in the present?

The real challenge for you in the fiction section is to read, in Thomas Foster's phrase, *like a professor*. How does a professor read? According to Foster, she relies on memory (who does this character remind me of and where have I seen this story before?), symbol (everything can be a symbol—but of what?), and pattern (man versus nature, boy meets girl, or, as Leslie Nielsen states it in *The Naked Gun*, "Same old story. Boy finds girl. Boy loses girl. Girl finds boy. Boy forgets girl. Boy remembers girl. Girl dies in tragic blimp accident over the Orange Bowl on New Year's Day.").

Read like a professor and you'll be ready to teach the class.

Come to Your Senses

We often miss the obvious because we dismiss easily. Study the poem below:

l(a

le
af
fa

ll

s)
one
l

iness

When e. e. cummings published this poem in 1958, the reviews were worse than those for the movie *Gigli*. Really. The critics thought it was stupid. According to Brown University professor Barry A. Marks, it looked "more like a picture of the Washington Monument or a telephone pole than a poem."

So why did Marks feel that the poem deserves our attention? Although the letters seem to have collided and the entire poem is less than a complete sentence, cummings sees what we do not. If you remove the parenthetical thought, what remains is the word "loneliness."

l

one
l

iness

Our eyes now see what cummings saw. The word "loneliness" reminds us of how alone we are by repeating one-one-one. As cummings teaches us, the letter "el" doubles as the figure "1." This repetition of meaning was always in the word "loneliness," but we didn't see it until cummings split the word for us.

In understanding works of literature, don't forget the importance of your senses. Writers, especially poets, occasionally place words on the page as if they were actors on a stage. You must recognize the "actor's blocking" to fully interpret the meaning.

Your hearing matters, too. Welsh poet Dylan Thomas loved the sounds of words. He was known to choose a particular word because it pleased his ear—what it actually meant in the context of

the poem was secondary. To appreciate some of his poems, therefore, they must be read aloud.

As for your sense of smell, listen to almost any of the rhyming
hip-hoppers that are so popular today. Now hold your nose. You
may think, of course, that criticism is unfair. What do you think
the average test maker would say about most of the things you
believe are "cool"? As we suggested earlier: open your eyes. The
irony is visible everywhere.

> I'd rather learn from one bird how to sing than teach ten
> thousand stars how not to dance.
>   —e. e. cummings

TEST
STRATEGIES

When you're on the Titanic, *you load the lifeboats. You don't stop to yell at the iceberg.*
   —Patricia Heaton, "Everybody Loves Raymond"

Think of the ACT as an iceberg. Think of the following ten strategies as your lifeboats.

Be the Test Maker

After all, what is reality anyway?
Nothing but a collective hunch.
—Lily Tomlin
Search for Signs of Intelligent Life in the Universe

OK, earning a high verbal score isn't exactly *Zen and the Art of Reading.* But you need to stop thinking as a test taker and start thinking as a test maker. If you could crawl inside the brain of the average test maker, you wouldn't find the next Ozzie Osbourne. You would find, instead, someone who is positive, patriotic, politically correct. What does that mean to you? You should give serious consideration to answers that reflect those qualities.

Be careful, though, of assuming too much. In his book *Sex, Drugs, and Cocoa Puffs,* Chuck Klosterman reveals the results of a study he conducted on the effects of patriotism. He sent out a mass e-mail to his acquaintances. In the e-mail he gave everyone two potential options for a hypothetical blind date. The respondents were instructed to pick whom they'd prefer. The first candidate was described as "attractive and successful." The second candidate was said to be "attractive, successful, and extremely patriotic." No other details were given.

Are you surprised to learn that just about everyone responded by selecting the first individual? Klosterman's point is that many of us are suspicious of the "too patriotic." E-mail respondents compared the second individual to Ted Nugent and Patrick Henry. One said that patriotic people weren't smart. The lesson for you? Don't go overboard.

Two Self-Evident Truths

1. **The average test maker is just a little bit afraid.** Do you actually believe that the the the folks at ACT want to argue about which of their answers are correct? Test makers can't afford to be second-guessed by thousands of enraged students who provide plausible alternative answers. Test makers, therefore, tend toward the obvious answer, the unarguable answer. You should too.

2. **Don't outsmart yourself.** The ACT does not reward the "star" of classroom discussions: the meaning-behind-the-meaning kid, the clever kid—in short, anyone with a personality.

Ah, the Humanity (etc.)

I had always planned on going to Columbia . . .
but they had tests to get in.
—Jon Stewart, "The Daily Show"

This just in for all of you fake news show hosts of the future: you still have to take tests. The ACT Reading test will ask you to read four passages, each about 750 words long, and answer ten questions on each passage. You've got to do all that in thirty-five minutes, which is just under ten minutes per passage. You're going to have to keep one eye on your watch as you work to pace yourself.

The passages will be taken from each of four areas: humanities, natural sciences, social sciences, and fiction. Passages in the humanities might include topics about the arts, movies, TV, literature, or philosophy. The natural science passages will cover just about every hard science you can think of, including astronomy, botany, geology, physics, and zoology. The social science section might include history, politics, or anything relating to people's behavior. Finally, the fiction section will include a short story or portion of a short story, novel, or memoir.

Pay special attention to the following discussion of these passages. Each type of passage offers a unique challenge.

Ah, the Humanity

The humanities passages are usually about art, literature, or philosophy. The focus is less on facts, more on inference. Consider what columnist Dave Barry has to say about the history of painting:

> After the Mother and Child Phase came the Enormous
> Naked Women Eating Fruit Phase, which was followed by
> the Just Plain Fruit with No Women of Any Kind Phase and
> the Famous Kings and Dukes Wearing Silly Outfits Phase.
> All of the phases were part of the Sharp and Clear School of
> painting, which means that even though the subjects were
> boring, they were at least recognizable. The Sharp and Clear
> School ended with Vincent Van Gogh, who invented the
> Fuzzy but Still Recognizable School and cut off his ear. This
> led to the No Longer Recognizable at All School, and finally
> to the Sharp and Clear Again but Mostly Just Rectangles
> School, which is the school that is popular today, except at
> shopping malls.

Now no one would accuse Barry of worrying about facts, but you can infer a thing or two from his insights. You won't find much in the way of great art at shopping malls, for example.

The most important thing to remember when reading these questions: *slow down*. Because some of the questions are based on inferences, you have to think about the implications of what you are reading. The good news is that these passages are almost always politically correct and positive. You are not likely to read a passage from an author asserting that Denzel Washington was overrated as an actor. Respond accordingly.

The ACT has been criticized in the past for insensitivity to minorities. If you come across a passage that discusses a minority issue, you can expect kid-glove treatment. In the ACT world, everything is beautiful in its own way.

To focus your thinking, you may want to jot down a few notes in the margin. (See Strategy 5 for suggestions.) If you can't separate the inferences, your hopes of answering the questions correctly could go up in flames.

And you don't want to be the next Hindenburg-er.

Houston, We Have a Passage

In a graduation talk for the UNC School of Information and Library Science, Martin Dillon's calculations demonstrated how trends and statistics can be dangerous. Evidently, the number of Elvis impersonators grew from 51 in 1981 to almost 15,000 in 1995. Dillon says, "If that trend continues, there will be some 50,000,000 Elvis impersonators in the U.S. alone by the year 2015. In the graduating class of that year, every 5th or 6th student would be an Elvis impersonator."

Elvis is not the only one who wants to leave the building. A natural science passage can be intimidating to anyone. Calculations discussed may be mind-boggling. The scientific jargon is often confusing. Fortunately, choosing the correct answer rarely depends on understanding a particular scientific term, and the calculations only matter on the Math section.

Any confusing scientific term will usually be explained in the sentences before and after it. For example, a question about "quarks" might seem difficult until you study that part of the passage that explains what a quark is. Since you have scanned the questions first (see Strategy 4), circle the word as you read the passage so you can find it later.

> Of the several hundred subatomic particles out of which
> physicists tell us all matter is made, the quark is the most
> evasive, the most piquing, and the most basic—so small as to
> have no size and so simple as to have no internal structure. Of

*course nobody's managed to shake a quark loose for closer
inspection (the most they've been able to do is to hit a few
over the head with beams of electrons), but that hasn't
stopped scientists from insisting that quarks, like black girl
groups of the Sixties, usually travel in threes and carry
electrical charges. . . .*
 —Judy Jones and William Wilson, *An Incomplete Education*

Remember: the answers to most of these questions are based on
the facts in the passage. Rarely do you have to address the inferences in the passage. And, Science marches on.

History Retreats Itself

"To be is to do." Socrates

"To do is to be." Jean-Paul Sartre

"Do be do be do." Frank Sinatra
 —Kurt Vonnegut Jr.

Here's to revisionist thinking! You've finally stumbled onto those
questions of mass destruction that you knew were there all the time.
   In the following social science passage, Robert Benchley describes
what has become a tense, and sometimes confusing, part of most
public meetings: "The Treasurer's Report."

*Now, in connection with reading this report, there are one or
two points which Dr. Murnie wanted brought up in
connection with it, and he asked me to bring them up in
connec—to bring them up.
    In the first place, there is the question of the work which we
are trying to do up there at our little place at Silver Lake, a*

*work which we feel not only fills a very definite need in the
community but also fills a very definite need—er—in the
community. I don't think that many members of the society
realize just how big the work is that we are trying to do up
there. For instance, I don't think that it is generally known
that most of our boys are between the age of fourteen. We feel
that, by taking the boy at this age, we can get closer to his real
nature—for a boy has a very real nature, you may be sure—
and bring him into closer touch not only with the school, the
parents, and with each other, but also the town in which they
live, the country to whose flag they pay allegiance—and to
the—ah—(trailing off) town in which they live.*

Although what happens in public meetings is an important part
of our history, these passages will generally be about a historical
trend or period. The historian's interpretation and supporting
examples are the source of the questions. Mark on the passage
when you come across this interpretation and the beginning of
each example (see also Strategy 5). A simple "I" and "E" would serve
this purpose. You can expect the historian to reference conflicting
opinions. You probably will be asked a question about this other
"disagreeable" historian as well. You might place a "C" next to this
argument.

. . . .

Tell Me a Story

These fiction passages are the most enjoyable to read. You may find
yourself saying, to borrow the unbridled enthusiasm of "The Daily
Show's" Jon Stewart, "It's smile-tastic. It's tickle-riffic." Then again,
maybe not.

*But all was not play at the University of Minnesota. Now I
began classes, and that was work—the good, satisfying work
of learning.*

I shall always remember the first class I attended. It was a class in sociology. I took a seat in the front row and spread my paper and pencils neatly on my desk. Turning to my brother students, I smiled friendlily. They threw lighted matches at me in a demonstration of good fellowship. Then the venerable white-haired professor entered the room. He advanced to the lectern at the head of the class. Putting on his pince-nez, he surveyed us for a moment. "Jeez," he said, "they get crumbier every year."

We laughed appreciatively.

In *Barefoot Boy with Cheek*, the author Max Shulman has his hero Asa Hearthrug laugh in the face of possible disaster. You, too, want to remain upbeat. So here is some advice about a fiction passage: don't rush through it. The questions will certainly address style and tone. You must be more aware of nuances in a fiction passage.

Warning: Do not read too much into your interpretation. You will not be rewarded for originality. Figure out the figurative language, but avoid overthinking your answers.

Mo, Hairy, and Curly Context

Moe: *Quiet!*
Larry: *I'm sorry, Moe. Please forgive me.*
Curly: *I'm trying to think but nothing happens.*

When you take the ACT, nothing happens more often than it does on reruns of "Seinfeld." This Strategy, on the other hand, gives you something to think about faster than you can say, "Hey Moe!" Generally, the questions on the Reading section fall into three Stooge-like categories.

I. Mo

These questions ask you about the "more," or the "Mo," of the passage, if you will. Some prep books call these the "Big Idea" or "Main Idea" questions.

> *I don't know. I mean, isn't Jake's impotence more about that generation's loss of faith in love?*
> —Rory, "Gilmore Girls"

In her English class at Yale, Rory defends her interpretation of Ernest Hemingway's novel *The Sun Also Rises*. Another student accuses Rory of ignoring the social context of underclass exploitation. What about World War I? Proving it's not always as easy as you think to find the bull in one of Hemingway's stories.

Fortunately, the "main idea" questions on the ACT are a little less debatable.

See if you can find Mo in the following passage:

> *If you really want to know what people in the United States are thinking about, you should write a letter to the editor. If you don't have time, National Public Radio's humorist Ian Shoales will do it for you. Here is an excerpt from one such letter that will please anyone regardless of political bent.*
>
> *"I realize this won't get printed in your so-called newspaper. The (Leftist, Conservative) slant is a disgrace to all (real Americans, taxpayers, our unborn children). Still I must urge everyone to (register to vote, write your Congressman, vote No on Prop 17) or we might not have (another four years, streetlights, a tomorrow).*
>
> *"As a (taxpayer, lifelong Democrat, home owner) I (view with alarm, am frightened by, am angered by) our (foreign policy, domestic policy, bleeding-heart environmentalists). Are we living in (a welfare state, Nazi Germany, a fool's paradise)?"*

You don't have to be in paradise to find the main idea in this passage. Shoales's willingness to write a letter for you is expressed near the beginning, the usual location for Mo. Some main ideas, however, are found later in the passage.

> *Tracy Ullman phones car dealers in Baltimore and comparison shops. Gary Oldman plays tapes on the freeway and ponders the uncanny congruities between Lee Harvey Oswald and Yogi Bear. Barbara Hershey tools through the Louisiana swamps and climbs ashore now and then for a chat.*
>
> *All these slightly undignified enterprises are dramatic research, simply the lengths to which some actors will go to find and perfect an acceptable accent.*

In this passage, Judith Shulevitz of the *New York Times* writes about the preparation process for some actors. The Mo is contained in the second paragraph following the examples discussed in the first paragraph. In the second paragraph, you learn that research to find an acceptable accent can be slightly undignified. The Mo.

....

2. Hairy

These questions can be trickier. The hairy part is finding the answer in the details of the passage. The hard questions are the ones where the answer is not apparent or, worse yet, hidden. You read more effectively when you read actively. Continually ask yourself: how do the supporting ideas link back to the main idea, the Mo? Sometimes that relationship is self-evident.

The young James Thurber, who later gained recognition as a cartoonist and humorist, struggled to win the approval of his editor. After the editor instructed Thurber to write short, dramatic leads, he produced the following:

> *Dead. That's what the man was when they found him with a knife in his back at 4:00 P.M. in front of Riley's saloon at the corner of 52nd and 12th streets.*

In this passage, Riley's saloon is a detail. In fact, all of the information about the crime scene could be described as supporting details. What it takes to write a dramatic lead is the implied main idea.

When you attack the longer passages, finding the details that answer a particular question can be more challenging. A question may ask you to draw an inference from a detail provided.

> *In* Life on the Mississippi, *Mark Twain, writing in 1874, observed that the lower part of the Mississippi River had been*

shortened 242 miles during the past 176 years—a little more
than a mile and a third each year.

From the details provided above you could infer that the Mississippi River would continue to shorten (unless measures were taken to change the course of history). If you read on, though, you discover that Twain's inferences are strikingly different from yours.

. . . any calm person who is not blind or idiotic can see that in
the Old Oolithic Silurian Period, just a million years ago next
November, the Lower Mississippi River was upward of one
million three hundred thousand miles long . . . And by the
same token any person can see that seven hundred and forty-
two years from now the Lower Mississippi will be only a mile
and three-quarters long.

Be careful. Don't assume too much, too quickly. And avoid the trap of trying to remember every single detail. These kinds of detail questions often refer to a specific line or paragraph. Fortunately, you can get the needed experience in finding details by completing the Practice Passages in this book.

....

3. Curly Context

Words are loaded pistols.
—Jean-Paul Sartre

Existentialism aside, Vocabulary in Context questions are the ones to unload first if you are running short on time. Sometimes the definition is fairly self-evident. The correct definition curls around the word to comfort you during your moment of need. Often, though, the test makers serve up a word with multiple definitions. You are given correct definitions for the word, but only one of those definitions works in context. You know the specific context because you will be given a line reference.

Warning: Don't rely on the common meaning for any word. The test makers will usually have a secondary definition among the choices. Just because an answer is true doesn't make it correct. For example, if you are asked about the word "skin," you might immediately think "epidermis." But the correct choice might be another meaning for that same word. As in, there's more than one way to skin a test maker.

Here are two examples to help you:

1. The words that curl around the term *Greek Chorus* state explicitly what you need to know.

   Greek plays were written in verse, like poetry, but the verse was close to the patterns of normal speech. The lines were spoken in unison by a chorus of people. The Greek Chorus consisted of members of the local population, and participation was considered a civic duty, much as voting is today.

2. Not all of the Vocabulary in Context questions, though, are that obvious.

   In the book Weird Wide Web, *authors Erfert Fenton and David Benton speculate on why there are so many web pages devoted to Spam. They wonder: "Is Hormel's canned meat product perhaps a metaphor for the Internet itself—made up of diverse elements, ubiquitous, and virtually indestructible?"*

   In this passage, the word *ubiquitous* means

   A. divergent
   B. omnipresent

C. carnivorous

D. cyberspace

You can eliminate the wrong choices fairly easily. An author is unlikely to repeat synonyms in a sentence structured to list different characteristics. Therefore, you can eliminate A (divergent). It is a synonym for the word *diverse* that is already a part of the list. The choice D (cyberspace) is the wrong part of speech (and it makes no sense in that sentence). Choice C (carnivorous) is there to fool you. The passage is about Spam. The Internet, however, is hardly a meat-eating entity. At least, not yet. The correct answer is B (omnipresent). The Internet is seemingly present everywhere. Watch out.

(conk) Woo woo woo woo woo woo woo woo woo woo, nyuk nyuk nyuk nyuk (bonk)
—Curly of "The Three Stooges"

The Questions Are the Answers

I have potential. Like I'm reading Moby Dick *and I'm not even halfway through and I can already tell you the ending. The whale is a robot. . . . Here's something I did not know. They number every page.*
—Michael Kelso, "That '70s Show"

They number every question, too. In one study, researchers found that students in colder states tended to do better on college admissions tests. Does that mean you should join Kelso in Wisconsin? Probably not, but you might want to consider the kinds of questions you'll be asked on the ACT.

For example, you'll find several general, or "big picture," questions. These questions investigate the theme, tone, or structure of a passage. Answer these first because they won't require you to look back. Then there are specific detail questions. Here you probably will need to return to the passage to find exactly the right answer. While you're there, you will want to look at vocabulary questions that test your ability to figure out the meaning of a word from its context. And finally, inference questions will ask you to read between the lines.

Consider these suggestions to make the most of your question-answering time.

1. Scan Can

You should scan the passages to focus your mind. Simply skim quickly for now. The purpose of this skimming is to find a topic that interests you. Begin with that passage. The higher your level of interest is, the stronger your start will be. If none of the topics grab you, then it's time for mind games. Convince yourself that you are fascinated by the subject matter. You would be surprised how revved-up you can get reading a scientific passage disproving the alternative hypothesis that the average raven is "clever"—especially if you are familiar with Monty Python's hypothesis that a "clever sheep" is dangerous. Let your mind be your friend.

2. Speed Kills

> *Aoccdrnig to rscheearch at an Elingsh uinervtisy, it deosn't mttaer in what oredr the ltteers in a wrod are, the olny iprmoetnt tihng is that the frist and lsat liteer are in the rghit pclae. The rset can be a toatl mses and you can sitil raed it wouthit a porbelm. Tihs is bcuseae we do not raed ervey lteter by itslef but the wrod as a wlohe and the biran fguiers it out aynawy.*
>
> —Phil Proctor, *Funny Times*

Some teachers contend that readers with the best comprehension are usually fast readers. The argument is based on the assumption that slow readers are more easily distracted. Daydream city, as it were. A more important concern, though, is how carefully you read the Reading passages.

In the movie *Reuben, Reuben*, the subject of speed-reading is raised. Academy Award nominee Tom Conti—who portrays a drunken, but brilliant poet—says that he would pay someone to teach him to read his favorite books as slowly as possible. Clearly, the poet in this film wants to savor every word.

Although you don't have time for much savoring, you should read as carefully as you can *and* still finish within the constraints of the exam.

3. Questions First

As you confront each new passage, read the questions first. Just the questions, not the answers. Too many conflicting answers can lead to information overload. In the middle of an important sentence, you don't want to find yourself wondering, "What was choice C anyway?"

You want increased focus rather than increased confusion. Some prep books disagree with this advice. These books argue that you may become so preoccupied with searching for answers that you will fail to get the overall meaning of the passage. To determine the best option for you, try using both methods on the Practice Passages in this book. Then stick with the system that works for you.

We recommend reading the questions first because reading comprehension is a two-step process: (1) perceiving and organizing information, and (2) connecting that information to what you already know. Your success in relating any information will increase if you have a frame of reference. The questions are that frame of reference. And those same questions should help you organize your thinking as you read through the passage.

Always remember that reading is an active process. Anticipate ideas. Your purpose is to actively search for the information you need to answer the questions you have already scanned. Have those questions in mind as you begin reading the passage. The search is about understanding. Don't worry about memorizing. Memorization is too time-consuming.

Tip: If you are running short of time, do the vocabulary in Curly context questions first, the Mo questions next, and the Hairy questions last.

4. Play the Odds

I used to be a gambler. But now I just make mental bets.
That's how I lost my mind.
    —Steve Allen

How much would you pay for all the secrets of the Universe? OK, what if we throw in the odds of guessing on the ACT? But wait. What if we send you an ice crusher? The truth is that you should guess. Unlike the SAT, there is NO penalty for guessing on the ACT.

When making difficult choices, former CIA director James Woolsey had his own way of determining the odds. Woolsey recalls the advice of the Damon Runyan character Harry the Horse. Runyan, a newspaperman in the 1920s, had Harry give this advice to gamblers: "Nothin' what depends on humans is worth odds of more than 8 to 5."

"IF HIS I.Q. IS BASED ON GUESSING THE RIGHT ANSWERS, PERHAPS WE COULD ASSUME HE'LL GO THROUGH LIFE BEING A REMARKABLY SUCCESSFUL GUESSER."

Context Messaging

To read between the lines was easier than to follow the text.
—Henry James

You don't have to read between the lines to know that students' reading skills have barely improved over the last decade. Clearly, few students are illiterate; too many, however, are "aliterate." These aliterate students can read, but they don't. And when they do, they are not fully engaged in the process. Such recalcitrance can affect how you approach those questions that refer you to specific words or lines in a passage. Read the following passage and answer the question that follows.

> In 1951, Oliver Brown, an African-American railroad worker 1
> from Topeka, Kansas, sued the city of Topeka for preventing
> his daughter from attending a local all-white school. Eight-
> year-old Linda Brown was forced to ride a bus for five miles
> when there was a school only four blocks from her home. 5
> The case, which went all the way to the Supreme Court
> (*Brown v. Board of Education*), challenged the constitutionality
> of an 1896 ruling, *Plessy v. Ferguson*. In *Plessy*, the court had
> decided that segregation was permissible as long as blacks
> and whites had access to "separate but equal" facilities. 10
>   Thurgood Marshall and his team of lawyers, though,
> presented evidence demonstrating that "separate but equal"
> was a logical impossibility. There could be no such thing as
> "separate but equal" facilities when society was arranged
> unequally. 15

In a 9–0 landmark decision, the Supreme Court ruled that segregated facilities degraded minorities and prevented them from having equal educational opportunities. As Chief Justice Earl Warren wrote, "Separate educational facilities are inherently unequal." *Plessy* was overturned. Although the 20 *Brown* decision applied only to education, it inspired minorities to seek rights in other fields, and it became a turning point in the civil rights movement.

Question: In lines 7–9, the importance of *Plessy* is addressed. The Supreme Court decision in *Brown v. Board of Education* affected this 1896 ruling by

A. challenging the constitutionality of *Plessy v. Ferguson*
B. becoming a turning point in the civil rights movement
C. changing "separate but equal" facilities
D. overturning *Plessy v. Ferguson*

Test makers can be tricky. If you skim the passage quickly or look only at lines 7 and 8, you might be tempted to choose A. The answer is true, but is it the best choice of the four? Later in the passage, you learn that the Supreme Court overturned *Plessy*. Ask yourself: does challenging the constitutionality of a ruling have a greater effect than overturning that ruling? No. Therefore, the correct answer is D. You could have quickly eliminated choice B because it doesn't deal specifically with *Plessy*. And choice C is simply not true.

Whenever the question refers you to specific lines in a passage, read the lines before and after to avoid such trickery. In the passage about *Brown v. Board of Education*, for example, you can heighten your interest by pretending that you really are Thurgood Marshall. And you have the opportunity to change this country for the better, but first you have to understand all of the facts of the case.

In other words, no matter what a passage is about, you should invest yourself in what is at stake. Make the outcome matter to you, and the outcome will be better for you.

Two Suggestions to Make That Investment Pay Off

1. **Be Noteworthy.** Taking notes on the passage can help some students. The simple act of noting a significant idea makes the next idea clearer for them. Circle important words. Underline key concepts. Comprehension, after all, depends upon understanding each preceding thought. But you have to be efficient. Develop an abbreviation code that works for you. You are not trying to write a book in the margins of the paper. You are merely highlighting what you hope will help you choose correct answers later.

   In *Parade*, Marilyn vos Savant discusses the potenial disadvantage of relying on such markings. Vos Savant says, "Some top students highlight elementary information; others note arcane material; still others mark abstruse sections; plenty make markings as idiosyncratic as their personalities."

   As always, time yourself on the Practice Passages. How much does it slow you down to make markings? Do those markings improve your ability to answer the questions correctly?

2. **Be Handy.** Once you've selected an answer, return to the place in the passage where you found the necessary information. Actually put your finger on that spot. Using your finger in this way decreases the chances that your fertile imagination is coming into play. Too often, the pressure of the moment takes over. The knowledge you brought to the testing site predis-

poses you to make certain choices. Your biases cut loose. You can't quite remember the words to the song that is stuck in your head.

Find the correct answer in the passage, not in the "Well, I've always thought" corner of your cerebrum, cerebellum, or medulla oblongata. When the ACT test is finally over, you don't want to say, "And that's all folks," like some Elmer be-Fudd-led.

The Night Before the Night Before

When a normal person goes to sleep they do not enter dream sleep for maybe 90 minutes after falling asleep. When narcoleptics like myself fall asleep we enter dream sleep right away. I am still awake when I begin to dream and I experience my dreams as hallucinations. Believe me, they are very, very real. If I dream that I got bit, I can feel it.
—Melody Zarnke, forty-five years old

In *Esquire*'s book *What It Feels Like*, one woman describes her narcolepsy. For some reason, the editors at *Esquire* did not include what it feels like to take the ACT. Strangely, though, the nightmarish qualities of the ACT are remarkably similar to what the woman reveals. And your understanding of sleep patterns can make a significant difference in your ability to perform well on the test.

Harvard medical researchers have concluded that a good night's rest consolidates memory. Furthermore, any successful coach will tell you that performance in competition is enhanced by resting well the night before the night before. Lack of sleep always catches up with you on the second day. In other words: sleep—plus practice—makes perfect.

In one particularly memorable episode of the animated television show "King of the Hill," Peggy Hill preps to participate in a book discussion group. Her efforts include memorizing pertinent facts about famous authors from an encyclopedia.

All right. Kafka. Kafka born 1883. Wore glasses. Burdened by
father. Loved to sleep in. Yes, Peggy, you are ready.

Even if you are unfamiliar with Franz Kafka's *The Metamorpho-*
sis, you don't want to wake up the morning before the ACT as a
cockroach. And it's certainly not the time to sleep in. Wake up! Star-
bucks awaits.

Be Happy, Be Healthy

Increasing evidence shows that personality, stress, and social life
can all influence your vulnerability to cold symptoms. Psycholo-
gist Sheldon Cohen of Carnegie-Mellon University in Pittsburgh
compares it to kindergarten: those who "play well with others" are
better off. What does this mean? Well, according to Marilyn Elias
in *USA Today*:

- Happy, relaxed people are more resistant to illness than
  those who tend to be unhappy or tense. And when happy
  people do get sick, their symptoms are milder.
- The more extroverted a person is, the less likely he is to
  catch cold.
- The longer people live with bad stress, the more likely they
  are to catch colds.

As you know, an exercise program can improve your state of
mind by reducing anxiety. Moreover, you will have more oxygen
getting to your brain, and you will be better able to think and to
concentrate. The extra energy you gain from regular physical
preparation will help sustain you during the latter parts of the
exam. If you take regular exercise breaks during your study peri-
ods before the exam, your productivity will increase. Endorphins
are your friends. Don't exercise, though, right before going to bed.
Such activity can make restful sleep difficult.

Finally, eat smart. Now is not the time to be a junk-food junkie. Consume the low-fat protein in fish, skinless poultry, beans, and legumes. Just say no to sugar and fat. These substances increase stress and lower immunity. Remember: Mom knows best. Ask her.

So all you really need to do is to change your entire personality. And make sure you get plenty of sleep the night before the night before.

Sweet dreams, slugabed.

Translate Questions into English

"Wheel of Fortune" was an important test prep for me.
—Mo Rocca, "The Daily Show"

In 1996, after thirteen successful years on "Wheel of Fortune," letter-turner Vanna White set a world record for the greatest quantity of apparel ever on television—5,500 outfits. A proud day for the entire White family. And what did she do on the show? Vanna White turned enough small boxes to reveal hidden letters that a discerning viewer would want to be disemvoweled.

But there is a lesson here. The hidden phrases that contestants must guess to win are quickly obvious to everyone in the audience and at home. Quick and obvious are good things, especially when you're under the pressure of a timed exam. Therefore, you should immediately translate all questions into words and phrases you recognize and understand. This translation is not always as easy as it sounds.

As a high school student, University of Chicago professor Austan Goolsbee discussed the potential for absurdity:

How do standardized tests judge your academic promise? Well, if you can define words like desuetude *and* lascivious, *then you have average potential. To rank at the top, you need to know words like* ouabain, *which is an African poison, or* schistosomiasis, *an endemic disease mentioned in the novel* Lord Jim. *I'll admit, such words may come in handy on a*

really boring date when you have nothing else to talk about,
but do they accurately reflect learning potential?

The truth is that the folks at ACT sometimes choose passages
that are unfamiliar. That makes sense. No student can possibly have
studied all known reading material before the exam. Unfortunately,
some obscure passages are steeped in language just as obscure.

Your task becomes, then, to translate that language into under-
standable ideas. In other words, *paraphrase.*

With a doff of the thinking cap to Edwin Newman's *On Lan-*
guage, let's practice on three statements that lack clarity.

> *1. In order to improve security, we request that, effective*
> *immediately, no employees use the above subject doors for*
> *ingress and egress to the building.*

In other words, don't open these doors.

> *2. The older man became an experiencing person in my life,*
> *lending an aura to my developing personality of absolute*
> *rapport and communicatory relevance.*

The older man was sympathetic and understanding.

> *3. The definition of net wage rate in equation (2) suggests*
> *that wage-rate changes are best parameterized by changes*
> *in u.*

Well . . . u are in big trouble . . . plus we all know how painful para-
meterizing can be.

There are, of course, other ways to get lost in the language
"bewilderness." A critical reader should be aware of euphemisms.
Writers sometimes substitute euphemisms for words that are harsh
or distasteful. Euphemisms often avoid the truth, lack clarity, and
are more evasive than helpful.

Pentagon officials are frequent winners of the "Doublespeak Award," which is given yearly to the individuals or groups that have done the most outstanding job of using language meant to "bamboozle and befuddle." Once, in the 1990s, the National Council of Teachers of English presented the award to the Defense Department for giving us an "armed situation"—not a war—in the Persian Gulf.

War is tough on words, according to the English teachers. The first Gulf War was rich in euphemisms, says William Lutz, a Rutgers University professor and chairman of the organization's Committee on Public Doublespeak.

For instance, bombing attacks against Iraq in 1991 were "efforts," and warplanes were "weapon systems." When pilots were on missions, they were "visiting a site." Buildings were "hard targets" and people were "soft" ones. Bombs didn't kill. They "degraded," "neutralized," "cleansed," or "sanitized." Killing the enemy was termed "servicing the target."

The allies were also guilty as charged by the teachers. The government of Saudi Arabia, unable to accept U.S. female soldiers, called them "males with female features."

Understand Overstatements

Always read something that will make you look good if you die in the middle of it.
—P. J. O'Rourke

So far, we've focused on reading the passages in the ACT exam. But there's something else that requires reading—the answers. Sometimes a careful reading of the answers could help you eliminate some contenders and leave the field clear for the winner.

Be on the lookout, for example, for overstatements ("everyone agrees," "she never does that," "all of us insist") and sweeping language that pushes aside any moderation or nuance. It's rare on the ACT that the correct answer would be so one-sided. Most of the passages are written by teachers or professors—people given to moderate, carefully considered opinions. Choices with extreme or exaggerated claims distort the real meaning of the passage.

In this passage, for example, on the *Lord of the Rings* movie trilogy, note answers B and D.

The basis of the movies is J. R. R. Tolkien's trilogy of Middle Earth books, themselves a reworking of similar ancient themes. For, in his writings, the scholarly Tolkien liberally lifted from myth, folklore, and ancient languages. The name "Middle Earth," for example, was either taken from Old English or from the Norse creation myth. The names of the dwarves, Gandalf, and other wizards were lifted from Snorri Sturluson's "Prose Edde," and Mordor, the evil enclave that

Frodo Baggins must traverse to deliver the ring to Mount Doom, is Old English for "murder."

Question: Which of the following best explains how Tolkien wrote *Lord of the Rings*?

A. Tolkien recycles ancient mythology and religion.
B. The characters and settings come entirely from his imagination.
C. The author uses his imagination to give new life to figures from folktales and literature of the Middle Ages.
D. Virtually every character and place name in *Lord of the Rings* comes from Norse myths or Old English stories.

Both B and D are too sweeping to do justice to Tolkien's true method. The correct answer, in case you're keeping score, is C.

Just as ACT passages tend to express moderate, carefully constructed positions, they also tend to focus on specific topics and that means you can rule out answers that sound too general. Choices with the wrong scope are either too broad or narrow in focus—either they're too general for the passage, or they focus too much on the details. Remember Goldilocks?

The first bowl of porridge she tried was too hot, the second too cool, and only the third just right. That's what you're looking for in a correct answer—something not too hot or too cold. Easier said than done, perhaps.

Finally, you should be wary of answers that seem correct in every respect—except that they contradict the passage. Often on the ACT, you'll find answers that sound OK but don't answer the question at all, or worse yet, they say the exact opposite of the correct answer. These answers sound reasonable, but they just don't fit the passage.

Such answers may be more tempting than you might think. They often have all the elements of a correct answer, and in the right order, but they insert a tiny word such as "not" or "no" and completely subvert the real meaning of the passage. For example, suppose the passage in question was this:

> *In the 1990s, when gambling on college sports became a*
> *major attraction at Las Vegas casinos, the betting action*
> *topped $2 billion a year, and the NCAA basketball*
> *championship rivaled the Super Bowl as the single largest*
> *gambling event. More college athletes were involved in fixing*
> *games or wagering on college teams than in any of the decades*
> *before legalized gaming became popular.*

Your question might be: what is the author's position on college athletes and gambling?

A wrong, but compelling answer might be: "College athletes are prohibited from gambling by the NCAA." That statement is true, but it hardly fits the passage. Worse yet, consider this answer: "College athletes are no longer in jeopardy because sports betting has been legalized in Las Vegas."

Alas, not true of life, not true of the passage.

Read as a Writer

When author Anna Quindlen was in the eighth grade, she took a scholarship test for a convent school. The essay test began with the quotation:

It is a far, far better thing that I do, than I have ever done; it is a far, far better rest that I go to, than I have ever known.

In her book *How Reading Changed My Life*, Quindlen describes how she knew that the scholarship was hers. "How many times had I gone up the steps to the guillotine with Sydney Carton as he went to that 'far, far better rest' at the end of *A Tale of Two Cities*?"

Quindlen, of course, went on to win a Pulitzer Prize and to become a bestselling author. But her journey began with a love for reading books. Long before she ever plugged in a word processor, she had made reading "her home, her sustenance." And she ate book after book. You should do the same. Furthermore, you should live within the pages of each book. You, too, can find yourself on the steps "to the guillotine with Sydney Carton."

But for a far, far better rest, you should try to think as Dickens did. As Quindlen does today. Read as a writer. Writing teacher Donald M. Murray reminds us that "the woman who plays basketball watches the game differently than the people around her, in the bleachers." What Murray means is that you need to become involved in the text as if you were the writer. A writer will study the Reading passages with a more critical eye.

Imagine the unwritten text before you. A writer must choose among a seemingly infinite number of words, scribbled notes, scattered memories, distracting thoughts, and so on. The writer takes those bits and pieces and puts them together to form meaning. If you approach each passage with the understanding that it once was an unwritten text, you have a better chance of deciphering the meaning of each phrase, sentence, and paragraph. You are, as Murray would argue, an archeologist sifting "through the refuse of an ancient civilization." You are searching for fragments of truth. Find those fragments and you can answer any question.

In the Foreword to the ACT Essay book in this series, Arthur Golden explains that context is everything. He states that a passage isn't beautiful "because of the writer's choice of words so much as because it draws together and draws upon, the material that comes before it." When you, as a reader, understand that those choices work collectively to create meaning, then you are well on your way to finding what is hidden. Study the following words of Seymour Glass, a character created by J. D. Salinger.

> *Certain heads, certain colors, and textures of human hair leave permanent marks on me. Other things too. Charlotte once ran away from me outside the studio, and I grabbed her dress to stop her, to keep her near me. A yellow cotton dress I loved because it was too long for her. I still have a lemon-yellow mark on the palm of my right hand. Oh, God, if I'm anything by a clinical name, I'm kind of a paranoic in reverse. I suspect people of plotting to make me happy.*

The Cliffs Notes interpretation would point out that certain things go unnoticed by most people. What else is there? Remember that Salinger made specific choices as a writer that can help you as a reader. You must, though, begin to think as a writer thinks. Look for the unexpected possibility. For example, consider two choices made for the Seymour Glass passage.

1. Why would Salinger have Seymour love a dress that was too long? Does this detail suggest the innocence of a female child?

2. Is it important that the dress is yellow? Does that color suggest a reason for a permanent mark, a scar?

When you ask those kinds of questions, you are thinking as Salinger might have—in context. The answers that Salinger would offer don't really matter now. Your reading life is richer already, just for the asking.

Be a Medi-Tater Tot

A man ought to read just as inclination leads him;
for what he reads as a task will do him little good.
—Samuel Johnson

Of course, Dr. Johnson never had to take the ACT. The prospect of this rite of passage might have convinced him to make an exception for our book. The triumph of experience over hope, he might say. In the "Introduction" to *The Best American Non-required Reading 2003*, the delightful Zadie Smith observes that the "task" of required reading is never done. She argues that "Tradition is a formative and immense part of a writer's world . . . but experiment is essential."

Smith makes an excellent point. While you are currently preparing to answer questions on the ACT, you are also preparing for a lifetime of reading. You should not let the forced nature of temporary ACT preparation sour you permanently. Make "experimenting" a part of your reading life and you will always know what Smith calls the "joy of nonrequiredness."

So start reading now.

Experiment

Dr. Tom Fischgrund's study of students who got perfect scores on the SAT found that those students read nearly twice as much as average academic achievers. Your ACT score will benefit by that same commitment. Surprisingly, though, it didn't seem to matter much what you read. No "must-read" books emerged from the study. The key was to read a lot.

We suggest, however, that you choose books that challenge you and make you think. The more consideration you give to the ideas presented in a book, the more understanding you will have when asked difficult questions about those ideas. Read as much as you can the month before the exam. No matter what you read, you will improve your comprehension skills.

About a week before the ACT, take a timed, full-length practice test, and not just the Reading section discussed in this book. This trial run will give you ample opportunity to assess what you still don't know and to take corrective measures. For the Reading errors you have made, review the applicable parts of this book. Start resting two days before the test.

Tip: Cramming the night before the exam is not as beneficial as meditating.

> *And remember—always breathe. Even if I stop, you keep*
> *breathing out there, all right? Keep breathing. In and out. In*
> *and out. In and out.*
> —Christopher Durang, *Laughing Wild*

Although the woman speaking in Durang's play is trying to find a way to keep "laughing wild amid severest woe," her advice is meaningful to you—especially as you confront the severest woes of the ACT. Relaxation and visualization can help you increase your chances for success.

····················
Relaxation

Find a quiet setting. Sit in a comfortable chair. Breathe. Breathe deeply. Fill your lungs with the pleasure of sweet air. Then exhale. Repeat. Sink lower into the chair. Close your eyes. Clear your mind. Let yourself begin to breathe easily and naturally.

If this exercise fails to relax you (or you find it silly), turn to professional help.

Perhaps the classic work on relaxation is based on studies at Boston's Beth Israel Hospital and Harvard Medical School. *The Relaxation Response* by Herbert Benson and Miriam Z. Klipper is a simple, mind-body approach to relieving stress. Also recommended is *The Relaxation & Stress Reduction Workbook* by Martha Davis et al. This 280-page workbook is jam-packed with specific techniques for the stressed-at-large.

Visualization

Once you are relaxed, you should begin to visualize succeeding on the ACT. Visualization is seeing images in your mind as vividly as possible. This technique is not magic. You are merely taking advantage of the natural process of thoughts. Your thoughts should create a matrix or a blueprint for your success. If we see in our imagination what we want, it is more likely to happen.

So after you are in a relaxed state of mind, concentrate on that image. See every detail; the institutional clock on the wall, the wooden desk, the number 2 pencils, the pink Mohawk haircut of the student sitting in front of you, the sounds, the smells—and not just from the student blocking your view. Try to feel your elation as you answer each question correctly. Know that joy now. Right now. Live in that moment. Trust your brain to respond.

Keep telling yourself, "I am relaxed. I can answer those questions." You may scoff at this advice but World Class athletes practice visualization. And it's not for fun. The athletes understand that picturing success increases their chances for success.

As Arthur Miller said in his play *Death of a Salesman*, "Attention must be paid."

PRACTICE PASSAGES

Chance favors the prepared mind.
—Louis Pasteur

On his MSNBC show "Hardball," Chris Matthews quoted Pasteur's observation about chance as a way of explaining his own good fortune in life. Good advice for you. Prepare your mind by practicing with the passages that follow.

Preparing for the Practice Passages

While you are practicing, take comfort in the fact that you don't have to study the 800-page book *G.O.A.T. (Greatest of All Time)*. This tribute to Muhammad Ali weighs seventy-five pounds and sells for $3,545. On the other hand, you might learn some important lessons from the life of Ali. Angelo Dundee, Ali's former trainer, reminds us: "You never get to go back in life." Therefore, make chance your friend. Prepare. Don't be the dope that gets roped.

Therefore, what can you expect when you reach the Reading passages?

- **Length.** The passages are all about 750 words long.
- **Content.** The passages are taken from four areas: the humanities, social sciences, natural sciences, and fiction. They can vary in style and may include narrative, argumentative, or expository elements.
- **Number of questions.** You can expect to find ten questions following each passage. In the practice passages you will find here, we have duplicated that format.
- **Additional material.** The passages may come packaged with introductions and footnotes. Don't skip over these items: they help provide context for the passage and can sometimes help you find the right answers.

*I know what you are going to ask
and the answer is unknown.*

Fiction

Passage I

Imagine that by some quirk you've arrived early for your astronomy class. As you're sitting at your desk waiting for the other students to arrive, you begin to think about something interesting you read in the textbook. That's the premise for this short story, "Questions Undeniable," by Antonia Welsch.

The astronomy textbook told me to look at my thumb.   1

A curious request for such a logical, efficient text, but folly be damned if I didn't go ahead and look at it anyway. The thumb appeared to be an oddly-shaped pink stub when singled out for serious analysis. I had bitten down the nail all   5
the way to its sensitive nub during hours of obsessive-compulsive depravity, or whatever causes one to do such things.

Not having a pacifier or "binkie" as other children, I sucked my thumb until long after the conventions of society   10
forced other toddlers to stop. At first the habit was cute and my mother couldn't go a day without bystanders staring at her daughter, the little girl with shining straight blonde hair. "Oh! Look at the little angel sucking her thumb!" they'd say, or "Isn't that precious?" As time passed it became odd—   15
something that caused scorn and reproach from others. People would simply gawk at my dear mother asking only with their stares, "Is that girl doing what I think she is?"

Eventually, after a few oppressive months of torture from my elementary school compatriots, I decided conformity   20 wasn't a bad stance at all, and I resigned myself to only allow the comfort in the quiet moments just before sleep.

The book went on, "The matter in your thumb came into existence within minutes of the beginning of the universe." I looked at the worn flesh, "Even the calcium in the bone and the iron in the blood were assembled inside stars." 25

"Assembled inside stars?" I stared apprehensively at the little appendage held out over my desk in the sparse classroom. "This thumb was built in a star?" My thoughts drifted from the thumb, which still smelled like salsa and chips from supper at the cafeteria, to the peach palm directly below it. 30 A tan bandage, worn from the day, was about ready to fall off, and pen marks gave hints to an afternoon filled with frenzied writing and random scribbles. "Not just my thumb, but all my parts, all of me were made in those places." My mind 35 raced with fantastic ideas: where had my little herd of molecules been? What had they been a part of? What had they witnessed in the immense span of time we call eternity?

"My atoms, they saw creation," I whispered, thinking back to those bible stories I had read as a child. An old man with 40 a long white beard and a big nose would say, "In the beginning . . ." This deity with wild hair and a cloud-woven shirt was not of my time or realm—He remained apart or above, speaking hard-to-understand words about harder-to-understand times. This passage from the astronomy book 45 was somehow different, though; it was alive with possibilities.

I read the words again, "assembled inside stars." Whimsical, isn't it? The words seemed to dance on my tongue. Particles that at one time floated through the vast emptiness of space, or violently exploded in a dazzling supernova, or 50 rained with meteor showers made up everything inside me.

More students wandered into the classroom. I kept my thumb in the same awkward "thumbs up" pose, though lowered it a bit so as not to cause alarm and confusion.

A new idea slipped quietly into my mind.   55

It didn't explode like a supernova, but crept slowly and softly into the gray matter. This thought was a small plant and I nurtured it, allowing it to grow and mature. As it took shape, it finally blossomed like flower petals glowing in June's sunshine.   60

The violet, crimson, and yellow blossoms, their atoms saw creation too. They flew across space just as mine did. Perhaps they traveled with my troupe of elements or maybe they were far ahead. Somehow, though, they got here—to this place, this section of the universe. These elements—   65 these building blocks of life could have comprised different forms before they came to be what is known as *I*. "Had I ever been a flower?" I gulped, "How could I know? For all I know I used to be a bad salami sandwich Mom ate in '83, or a poem by Longfellow."   70

Looking down at the yellow wood of my desk I noticed the graphic remarks and drawings scribbled about, suggesting both the vulgarity and wit of past students. "Will this battered chair be the next Einstein? Or even Shakespeare? Could these atoms be some future abused wife, or orphaned   75 child?" I looked up and saw other students sitting in their desks trying to read the chapter before class began.

At least half were looking strangely at their thumbs.

"That's it, isn't it?" I muttered under my breath, careful not to attract unwanted attention. "If we are made of the uni-   80 verse," hesitating, I collected my thoughts in an attempt to see through the fog of philosophic pursuits, "if we are made of the universe—the flower petals, and thumbs, and atoms that comprise the matter of what we call the universe, and every Monday and Tuesday night we sit here and try to   85 understand the concepts, rules, and forces of astronomy, then are we, or are we not, the universe trying to understand itself?" All the air left my body as though I had been suddenly punched in the stomach. I couldn't help but look alarmed. The girl next to me looked stunned as well—as did every- 90 one who had overheard my little revelation.

I was barely aware of the professor standing next to me.

"Looks like you've hit on something, Miss." He smiled, "And it is an engaging thought, isn't it?"

"Yes, I, uh . . ." 95

Winking, he turned and walked up to the podium in order to start class. My gaze shifted from him, to my thumb, slowly down to the text, and back to my thumb. "I guess it is," I said.

I felt small and comfortable and eternal as the sound of opening notebooks and laughter bounced off the planetar- 100 ium walls. He went on with class that day as usual, discussing other mysteries far beyond my little brain's comprehension, going over the ferocious beauty of stars millions of light years away. Now I was a part of that. I was and am irrevocably con-nected to the universe in a personal way I hadn't thought 105 possible. Through it all, through the lecture and lab, I didn't dare take my eyes off that thumb—with all its billions of wondrous atoms looking back—for in it, I could see eternity.

Questions

Question 1: Name one of the undeniable questions referred to in the title of the story.

A. What is the universe made of?
B. What is our purpose?
C. Why study astronomy?
D. Is the Bible true?

Question 2: Why does the narrator have ambivalent feelings about her thumb?

A. It seems odd that an astronomy textbook would ask students to look at thumbs.

B. While other children had pacifiers, she had to make do by sucking her thumb.

C. She thinks her thumb is ugly because she chews her nails.

D. Although she took some comfort from sucking her thumb, others made fun of her.

Question 3: The narrator's memory of her thumb sucking seems like a digression at first, a departure from the main point of the story. But upon further reflection, this anecdote may act as a preview for her larger point. What did the narrator learn from her "thumb" experiences?

A. People can be cruel.

B. She had to set aside some comfortable answers as she got older for more socially accepted ones.

C. Thumb-sucking should be considered acceptable behavior.

D. Conformity is okay after all.

Question 4: Which is the best explanation for what is meant by the phrase, "This thumb was built in a star."

A. Atoms—the stuff the universe is made of—are the same as they have always been.

B. The narrator has been reading too many science fiction books.

C. Particles have been shooting through space for eons.

D. Meteor showers brought new elements to earth.

Question 5: Which of these statements does not accurately describe the narrator's thumb?

A. It smells of salsa.

B. It seems oddly shaped.

   C. It is unusually long and slender.
   D. The nail has been bitten down to the quick.

Question 6: The narrator tries to draw a contrast between the theory she finds in her astronomy textbook for the origin of the universe and

   A. scientific accounts in other fields such as geology
   B. what several of her classmates have told her
   C. the account of creation in the Bible
   D. what her mother used to say

Question 7: As the other students begin to filter into class, the narrator does something to avoid calling attention to herself. She

   A. turns her thumb to the "thumbs down" position
   B. lowers her thumb
   C. crosses her hands
   D. puts her hands in her lap below the desktop

Question 8: The narrator uses a metaphor, a simile to be specific, to describe a mental image she has of her idea. She compares her idea about the building blocks of the universe to

   A. a meteor shower
   B. a classroom desk covered with graffiti
   C. a supernova
   D. the petals of a flower

Question 9: What does the narrator say she has in common with a salami sandwich?

   A. Both are important to her mother.
   B. Both originated in 1983.

C. Both are made up of atoms.

D. Both help explain the universe.

Question 10: How does the professor feel about the narrator's discovery?

A. He's pleased she is thinking about the material.

B. He's irritated that she talks to herself during class.

C. He's amazed she finished the reading assignment.

D. He's amused at the simplicity of her idea.

Answers

1. A 2. D 3. B 4. A 5. C 6. C 7. B 8. D 9. C 10. A

Commentary

All the answers for Question 1 are rich, philosophical issues, but the only one that is directly relevant to this story is A, "What is the universe made of?" The narrator's quest is to understand what her thumb has in common with flowers, a wooden desk, and supernovas—the answer, she reasons, is atoms. Question 2 contains a key vocabulary term in the question, not the answers. You need to know that "ambivalent" means twofold, or mutually conflicting feelings (think of "ambidextrous" or "ambiguous" for clues). Question 3 is a bit tricky because it asks you to see a larger pattern prefigured in a small story. The point of the narrator's thumb-sucking memory is that the old comfortable answers may not work as one becomes an adult. For Question 4, you must read beyond the first mention of the phrase, "assembled inside stars," all the way to where that phrase is mentioned again three paragraphs later—the answer can be found between the two references.

Questions 5, 6, and 7 may require that you return to the passage for close inspection (all the questions require you to identify a detail). In question 8, if you can remember that a simile requires the use of "like" or "as," you should be able to easily find this: "it finally blossomed like flower petals." Question 9 is consistent with many references throughout the passage where the narrator reasons that the same atoms she finds in her thumb can be found in desks, poems, and even sandwiches. We know in question 10 that the professor is pleased by what the narrator has said out loud because he smiles and says something encouraging to her.

Passage 2

An enduring classic, My Antonia *by Willa Cather is the unforgettable story of an immigrant woman's life on the hardscrabble Nebraska plains.*

On the afternoon of that same Sunday I took my first long   1
ride on my pony, under Otto's direction. After that Dude
and I went twice a week to the post office, six miles east of
us, and I saved the men a good deal of time by riding on
errands to our neighbors. When we had to borrow anything,   5
or to send about word that there would be preaching at the
sod schoolhouse, I was always the messenger. Formerly
Fuchs attended to such things after working hours.

All the years that have passed have not dimmed my memory of that first glorious autumn. The new country lay open   10
before me: there were no fences in those days, and I could
choose my own way over the grass uplands, trusting the
pony to get me home again. Sometimes I followed the sunflower-bordered roads. Fuchs told me that the sunflowers
were introduced into that country by the Mormons; that at   15
the time of the persecution, when they left Missouri and
struck out into the wilderness to find a place where they
could worship God in their own way, the members of the
first exploring party, crossing the plains to Utah, scattered
sunflower seed as they went. The next summer, when the   20
long trains of wagons came through with all the women and
children, they had the sunflower trail to follow. I believe that
botanists do not confirm Fuchs's story, but insist that the
sunflower was native to those plains. Nevertheless, that leg-

end has stuck in my mind, and sunflower-bordered roads 25
always seem to me the roads to freedom.

I used to love to drift along the pale-yellow cornfields,
looking for the damp spots one sometimes found at their
edges, where the smartweed soon turned a rich copper 30
color and the narrow brown leaves hung curled like cocoons
about the swollen joints of the stem. Sometimes I went south
to visit our German neighbors and to admire their catalpa
grove, or to see the big elm tree that grew up out of a deep 35
crack in the earth and had a hawk's nest in its branches. Trees
were so rare in that country, and they had to make such a
hard fight to grow, that we used to feel anxious about them,
and visit them as if they were persons. It must have been the 40
scarcity of detail in that tawny landscape that made detail so
precious.

Sometimes I rode north to the big prairie-dog town to
watch the brown earth owls fly home in the late afternoon 45
and go down to their nests underground with the dogs.
Antonia Shimerda liked to go with me, and we used to wonder a great deal about these birds of subterranean habit. We
had to be on our guard there, for rattlesnakes were always 50
lurking about. They came to pick up an easy living among the
dogs and owls, which were quite defenseless against them;
took possession of their comfortable houses and ate the
eggs and puppies. We felt sorry for the owls. It was always 55
mournful to see them come flying home at sunset and dis-
appear under the earth. But, after all, we felt, winged things
who would live like that must be rather degraded creatures.
The dog-town was a long way from any pond or creek. Otto 60
Fuchs said he had seen populous dog-towns in the desert
where there was no surface water for fifty miles; he insisted
that some of the holes must go down to water—nearly two
hundred feet, hereabouts. Antonia said she didn't believe it; 65
that the dogs probably lapped up the dew in the early morning, like the rabbits.

Antonia had opinions about everything, and she was soon able to make them known. Almost every day she came running across the prairie to have her reading lesson with me. Mrs. Shimerda grumbled, but realized it was important that one member of the family should learn English. When the lesson was over, we used to go up to the watermelon patch behind the garden. I split the melons with an old corn-knife and we lifted out the hearts and ate them with the juice trickling through our fingers. The white Christmas melons we did not touch, but we watched them with curiosity. They were to be picked late, when the hard frosts had set in, and put away for winter use. After weeks on the ocean, the Shimerdas were famished for fruit.

Questions

Question 1: The narrator characterizes his worth to the community as a

- A. botanist
- B. teacher
- C. messenger
- D. Mormon

Question 2: Who is Dude?

- A. a local cowhand
- B. a recent immigrant
- C. the narrator's horse
- D. the previous messenger

Question 3: The narrator explains the legend of the sunflower trail, but also tells the reader that botanists say that sunflowers are native to the area. The conclusion the narrator draws is that

A. we should put our faith in science
B. in spite of science, we can enjoy the romantic image of the legend
C. the Mormons took another route
D. legends are just for children

Question 4: For the narrator, the roads to freedom were

A. so precious
B. just a dream
C. through yellow cornfields
D. sunflower-bordered

Question 5: The pioneers in this passage had a special feeling about trees: they took an intense interest in them, almost as if they were persons. Why?

A. They were so rare.
B. They provided important resources such as food and timber.
C. There was so little else to look at.
D. There weren't enough people around to care about.

Question 6: Which two adjectives best describe the narrator?

A. observant/carefree
B. curious/responsible
C. adventurous/demure
D. frivolous/mournful

Question 7: Prairie dogs and earth owls had a common enemy:

A. each other
B. human predators

C. coyotes

D. rattlesnakes

Question 8: According to the narrator, Mrs. Shimerda wanted Antonia to have reading lessons because

A. she wanted Antonia to be more like the narrator

B. curiosity was important to her

C. education was necessary to succeed in America

D. someone in the family should learn English

Question 9: Surviving in the new world of America required all of the following from immigrant families except:

A. making friends with their neighbors

B. setting food aside to save for the long winter

C. learning to speak English

D. gaining citizenship status as quickly as possible

Question 10: All of the following are true about Antonia except:

A. she believed Otto about the populous dog-towns

B. she had opinions about everything

C. she was famished for fruit

D. she liked to wonder about brown earth owls

Answers

1. C 2. C 3. B 4. D 5. A 6. B 7. D 8. D 9. D 10. A

Commentary

In Question 1, C is correct. The other choices are mentioned in the story but do not apply to the narrator. A close reading of the passage will tell you that Dude, in Question 2, must be the narrator's horse because he is the means of his traveling six miles twice a week to the post office. Question 3 requires you to see that the narrator puts value in the legend even though he realizes it is more a fable than truth. First he tells the reader about the legend, then he brings up what science has to say, and finally, he returns to the enduring value of the legend.

The correct answer for Question 4 is found in the last sentence of the second paragraph—choice D. The comment that trees are remarkably rare on the high plains gives you the answer for Question 5. The key to Question 6 is finding a pair of adjectives that are both true. Only choice B meets this standard. For Question 7, the phrase "[rattlesnakes] pick up an easy living among the dogs and owls" in the passage tells you that the rattlesnakes prey on both dogs and owls. All of the choices in Question 8 may be true, but only D is stated explicitly in the text. In Question 9, use the process of elimination to find the right answer. All answers, except for D (gaining citizenship), are explicitly mentioned in the text. For Question 10, even though choice C is constructed differently than the other choices, it is not correct. The correct choice is A. Antonia has her own theory about the dog-towns.

Natural Sciences

Passage 3

The Hot Zone by Richard Preston tells the dramatic story of Ebola, a virus that kills nine out of ten of its victims so quickly and gruesomely that even biohazard experts are terrified. As the tropical wildernesses of the world are destroyed, previously unknown viruses that have lived undetected in the rain forest for eons are entering human populations.

A virus is a small capsule made of membranes and proteins.   1
The capsule contains one or more strands of DNA or RNA,
which are long molecules that contain the software program
for making a copy of the virus. Some biologists classify viruses
as "life forms" because they are not strictly known to be   5
alive. Viruses are ambiguously alive, neither alive nor dead.
They carry on their existence in the borderlands between
life and nonlife. Viruses that are outside cells merely sit there;
nothing happens. They are dead. They can even form crys-
tals. Virus particles that lie around in blood or mucus may   10
seem dead, but the particles are waiting for something to
come along. They have a sticky surface. If a cell comes along
and touches the virus and the stickiness of the virus matches
the stickiness of the cell, then the virus clings to the cell. The
cell feels the virus sticking to it and enfolds the virus and   15
drags it inside. Once the virus enters the cell, it becomes a
Trojan horse. It switches on and begins to replicate.

A virus is a parasite. It can't live on its own. It can only
make copies of itself inside a cell using the cell's materials
and machinery to get the job done. All living things carry   20

viruses in their cells. Even fungi and bacteria are inhabited by viruses and are occasionally destroyed by them. That is, diseases have their own diseases. A virus makes copies of itself inside a cell until eventually the cell gets pigged with virus and pops, and the viruses spill out of the broken cell. Or 25 viruses can bud through a cell wall, like drips coming out of a faucet—drip, drip, drip, drip, copy, copy, copy, copy—that's the way the AIDS virus works. The faucet runs and runs until the cell is exhausted, consumed, and destroyed. If enough cells are destroyed, the host dies. A virus does not "want" 30 to kill its host. That is not in the best interest of the virus, because then the virus may also die, unless it can jump fast enough out of the dying host into a new host.

The genetic code inside Ebola is a single strand of RNA. This type of molecule is thought to be the oldest and most 35 "primitive" coding mechanism for life. The earth's primordial ocean, which came into existence not long after the earth was formed, about four and a half billion years ago, may well have contained microscopic life forms based on RNA. This suggests that Ebola is an ancient kind of life, per- 40 haps nearly as old as the earth itself. Another hint that Ebola is extremely ancient is the way in which it can seem neither quite alive nor quite unalive.

Viruses may seem alive when they multiply, but in another sense they are obviously dead, are only machines, subtle ones 45 to be sure, but strictly mechanical, no more alive than a jackhammer. Viruses are molecular sharks, a motive without a mind. Compact, hard, logical, totally selfish, the virus is dedicated to making copies of itself—which it can do on occasion with radiant speed. The prime directive is to replicate. 50

Viruses are too small to be seen. Here is a way to imagine the size of a virus. Consider the island of Manhattan shrunk to the size of a tiny dot, just barely large enough to see. This Manhattan could easily hold nine million viruses. If 55 you could magnify this Manhattan and if it were full of viruses, you would see little figures clustered like the lunch crowd on Fifth Avenue. A hundred million crystallized polio viruses could cover the period at the end of this sentence. There could be 250 Woodstock Festivals of viruses sitting 60 on that period—the combined populations of Great Britain and France—and you would never know it.

Ebola is a rather simple virus—as simple as a firestorm. It kills humans with swift efficiency and with a devastating range of effects. Ebola is distantly related to measles, mumps, and 65 rabies. It is also related to certain pneumonia viruses: to the parainfluenza virus, which causes colds in children, and to the respiratory syncytial virus, which can cause fatal pneumonia in a person who has AIDS. In its own evolution through unknown hosts and hidden pathways in the rain forest, Ebola 70 seems to have developed the worst elements of all the above viruses. Like measles, it triggers a rash all over the body. Some of its effects resemble rabies—psychosis, madness. Other of its effects look eerily like a bad cold.

Questions

Question 1: The author refers to a virus as a Trojan horse because

    A. viruses often begin in farm animals
    B. the particles have a sticky surface
    C. it tricks a cell into dragging it inside
    D. it is also Greek to him

Question 2: The Ebola virus can best be described as a

    A. cell
    B. fungus
    C. parasite
    D. bacteria

Question 3: A virus is a strange life form, not quite dead or alive. A virus can seem dead because

A. it can't live on its own
B. it can kill its host
C. it is so ancient
D. it can make copies of itself

Question 4: All of the following are true about a virus except:

A. they seem alive when they multiply
B. Ebola is a complex virus
C. the genetic code inside Ebola is a single strand of RNA
D. they inhabit fungi and bacteria

Question 5: The most "primitive" coding mechanism for life is

A. RNA
B. DNA
C. AIDS
D. EBOLA

Question 6: You can infer from the passage that if viruses could think, they would prefer that their host

A. develop a cold
B. live
C. die
D. replicate itself

Question 7: The term "prime directive" most nearly means

A. careful instruction
B. prepare for pouring

C. most important duty
D. Spock is illogical

Question 8: To help people better grasp the tiny size of a virus particle, the writer compares the virus to the island of Manhattan, a lunch crowd on Fifth Avenue, and 250 Woodstock Festivals. Why did he choose those examples?

A. for humor
B. most of his readers live in New York
C. for emotional appeal
D. these are familiar images to American readers

Question 9: One can infer from this passage that

A. a virus is not a parasite
B. viruses are easily seen
C. a virus is a motive with a mind
D. a virus does not "want" to kill its host

Question 10: Ebola is related to a host of contagious illnesses. They include all of the following except:

A. mumps
B. hepatitis
C. pneumonia
D. measles

Answers
1. C 2. C 3. A 4. B 5. A 6. B 7. C 8. D 9. D 10. B

Commentary

The "Trojan horse" in Question 1 refers, of course, to the famous wooden horse left by the Greeks as an offering to their enemies, the Trojans. After the Trojans had dragged the horse within the city walls and fallen drunkenly asleep after celebrating their victory over the Greeks, the Greek soldiers, cleverly hidden inside the horse, slipped out and routed their rivals. The use of a Trojan horse as a metaphor for a virus is apt because the virus is inert until dragged inside a cell, where it begins to wreak its damage.

Careful reading will help you solve Question 2 as you discover that Ebola is a parasite. Questions 3 and 4 require you to work by eliminating the wrong answers. If you can get the number of possible answers down to two, guess away. Remember that unlike the SAT, wrong guesses won't hurt you on the ACT (and correct guesses will pay off). Question 5 requires you to draw information from two sentences, the two at the beginning of the third paragraph. Question 6 requires you to reverse one of the author's statements. The passage states that a virus does not "want" to kill its host; therefore, we can infer that if a virus could "think," it would prefer that its host survive. For Question 7, pick up contextual clues from previous sentences where we learn that viruses only seem to be alive when they multiply, that they are driven by a single motive, and that they are totally selfish. Putting these clues together, you can surmise that "prime directive" means "most important duty."

Question 8 requires a judgment call because all four answers are true to some degree. Your challenge is to find the best answer—D (familiar images to Americans). There's nothing especially humorous or emotional about a lunch crowd on Fifth Avenue, and although Fifth Avenue is located in New York, you would hardly expect most of the author's readers to live there. Question 9 asks you to draw a conclusion from the entire passage. Question 10 requires careful reading—you'll almost certainly have to go back to the passage for a quick check.

Passage 4

From Football Physics *by Timothy Gay*

The first, most basic instruction coaches give players about 1
tackling an opponent goes something like this: "Keep your
feet apart, stay low with your head up, and drive upward and
through the opposing player." In order to understand why
this technique is so effective, we now take up two new
physics ideas: the center of mass and torque. 5

Let's consider torque first. Simply put, torque is the rotational equivalent of force. In the same way that force causes
a mass to accelerate along a straight line, torque causes
objects to rotate about a pivot line, sometimes called the
axis of rotation. The bigger the torque, the more effective it 10
is at causing the object to which it is applied to rotate about
its pivot line.

We can illustrate these concepts by considering the simple act of opening a door. The door rotates about its pivot
line, defined by its hinges. Let's now apply a force of, say, five 15
pounds to the door, with the direction of the force being
perpendicular to the plane of the door. If the door is three
feet wide, and we apply the force at its edge farthest away
from the hinges, the lever arm of this force is three feet. The
torque we apply to the door is three feet × five pounds = 20
fifteen pounds–force feet (lbf × ft). Alternatively, we can
apply the same perpendicular force to the door, but now at
a distance of 0.1 foot from the hinges. Now the lever arm is
0.1 foot, and the applied torque is 0.5 lbf × ft. Which torque
is more effective in opening the door? It doesn't take Tom 25
Landry to figure this one out—it's the first one. The value
of applied torque is simply a quantitative measure of how
effectively the force we're applying opens the door.

Now consider a different possibility. We'll apply five
pounds of force to the door as before, and we'll apply it to 30
the edge of the door farthest from the hinges, just as before.

But now we change the direction of the applied force so that it points directly through the pivot line, parallel to the plane of the door. Common sense tells us that now the force we've applied isn't at all effective at opening the door. How does this relate to the torque? The lever arm of the force is now zero, because the force direction extends through the hinges themselves. Thus, the torque is zero; that door isn't going anywhere.

Torque by itself doesn't tell us much about tackling unless we combine it with an understanding of a player's center of mass. An object's center of mass is essentially the point through which we consider the pull of gravity on that object to act. This is why the center of mass is also referred to as the center of gravity. Most people have a basic concept of where the center of mass of an object lies—roughly at the object's center. And most people know that the admonishment "Keep your center of mass low!" means, roughly translated, "Crouch down, you!" This isn't wrong, but in order to really understand the center of mass, we need to determine the "center" of an object a little more carefully.

A player's center of mass is roughly just below his rib cage, on his vertical center line. When a player assumes a wide stance and crouches down to make a hit, his center of mass lowers (but remains in his torso area). If we constructed his helmet of lead, the center-of-mass point would move up perhaps an inch, because his head area would now be heavier. If we put the same amount of lead in his shoes (and how many of us haven't seen linemen who seemed to have this problem?), his center of mass would move down a few inches.

Here's the bottom line. When tackling or blocking, the reason to stay low and drive upward through the opposing player is so that you can control his motion by exerting far more torque on him than he does on you. Newton's Third Law still holds. You exert the same force on him as he does on you, but by using your knowledge of the centers of mass, you can completely dominate him in terms of torque.

Questions

Question 1: The scientific term *torque* means

A. a quantitative measure
B. the axis of rotation
C. a rotational force
D. the pivot line

Question 2: To illustrate the effects of torque, the author uses the example of

A. closing a door
B. making a tackle
C. accelerating along a straight line
D. opening a door

Question 3: The mathematical units used in the passage to measure torque are

A. force pounds per foot
B. pounds–force feet
C. feet
D. pounds

Question 4: To really understand tackling, a football player should grasp not only torque but also

A. center of mass
B. the pull of gravity
C. how to crouch
D. the importance of acceleration

Question 5: A player can lower his center of mass by

A. taking harder courses
B. assuming a wide stance

C. adjusting his shoulder pads
D. replacing his helmet

Question 6: The author makes a joke about filling helmets and football shoes with lead to illustrate which point?

A. we need to be careful when determining the center of an object
B. to find the center of mass, look along the vertical center line
C. that a player's center of mass is just below his rib cage
D. that the center of mass can be raised or lowered

Question 7: A player who applies proper physics can block or tackle successfully by

A. applying the same amount of force as his opponent
B. by using his torque to overcome the other player
C. staying low
D. applying Newton's Third Law

Question 8: The author uses a mathematical formula (distance times force) to

A. give his argument scientific validity
B. deliberately confuse the student
C. satisfy sports fans who love statistics
D. determine whether football coaches are right

Question 9: The author implies that some linemen are slow. He does this by saying that

A. some linemen have a high center of mass
B. some linemen have lead in their shoes
C. football coaches have to keep yelling at their players
D. linemen in a crouch can't run very fast

Question 10: Taking the passage as a whole, the author thinks the football coach's advice in the first sentence is

A. correct
B. false
C. misguided
D. missing the point

Answers

1. C 2. D 3. A 4. A 5. B 6. D 7. B 8. A 9. B 10. A

Commentary

In Question 1, you need to recognize that "rotation" is the key word in a definition of torque. That cuts the possible answers down to B and C. C is correct because torque is a way to describe "force." The author develops the example of opening a door throughout paragraphs three and four, so you shouldn't have trouble recognizing that in Question 2. Question 3 will probably send you back to the passage where you could check your memory of the mathematical units. Question 4 is answered in the first paragraph and repeated at the beginning of the fifth paragraph, and repeated one final time in the last paragraph. Applying a little common sense and reflecting on what the author has indicated about center of mass should help you solve Question 5.

In Question 6, all the answers are correct, but D is the most relevant to the author's purpose. The answer to Question 7 can be found in the last paragraph. Questions 8 and 10 refer to the overall point of the passage—do football coaches give good advice about tackling? Question 9 requires you to notice how the tone of the passage shifts—largely signaled by the presence of parentheses—when the author makes a small joke.

Humanities

Passage 5

From How I Discovered Words: A Homemade Education *by Malcolm X*

It was because of my letters that I happened to stumble upon   1
starting to acquire some kind of a homemade education.

I became increasingly frustrated at not being able to
express what I wanted to convey in letters that I wrote,
especially those to Mr. Elijah Muhammad. In the street, I had
been the most articulate hustler out there—I had com-   5
manded attention when I said something. But now, trying to
write simple English, I not only wasn't articulate, I wasn't even
functional. How would I sound writing in slang, the way I
would say it, something such as, "Look, daddy, let me pull
your coat about a cat, Elijah Muhammad—"   10

Many who today hear me somewhere in person, or on
television, or those who read something I've said, will think
I went to school far beyond the eighth grade. This impression is due entirely to my prison studies. It had really begun
back in the Charlestown Prison, when Bimbi first made me   15
feel envy of his stock of knowledge. Bimbi had always taken
charge of any conversation he was in, and I had tried to emulate him. But every book I picked up had few sentences
which didn't contain anywhere from one to nearly all of the
words that might as well have been in Chinese. When I just   20
skipped those words, of course, I really ended up with little
idea of what the book said. So I had come to the Norfolk

Prison Colony still going through only book-reading motions.
Pretty soon, I would have quit even these motions, unless I
had received the motivation that I did.   25

I saw that the best thing I could do was get hold of a dictionary—to study, to learn some words. I was lucky enough
to reason also that I should try to improve my penmanship.
It was sad. I couldn't even write in a straight line. It was both
ideas together that moved me to request a dictionary along   30
with some tablets and pencils from the Norfolk Prison
Colony school.

I spent two days just riffling uncertainly through the dictionary's pages. I'd never realized so many words existed! I
didn't know which words I needed to learn. Finally, just to   35
start some kind of action, I began copying. In my slow,
painstaking, ragged handwriting, I copied into my tablet
everything printed on that first page, down to the punctua-
tion marks. I believe it took me a day. Then, aloud, I read back,
to myself, everything I'd written on the tablet. Over and over, 40
aloud, to myself, I read my own handwriting.

I woke up the next morning, thinking about those words
—immensely proud to realize that not only had I written so
much at one time, but I'd written words that I never knew
were in the world. Moreover, with a little effort, I also could 45
remember what many of these words meant. I reviewed the
words whose meanings I didn't remember. Funny thing, from
the dictionary's first page right now, that "aardvark" springs
to my mind.

The dictionary had a picture of it, a long-tailed, long-eared, 50
burrowing African mammal, which lives off termites caught
by sticking out its tongue as an anteater does for ants. I was
so fascinated that I went on—I copied the dictionary's next
page. And the same experience came when I studied that.
With every succeeding page, I also learned of people and   55
places and events from history. Actually the dictionary is like
a miniature encyclopedia. Finally the dictionary's A section

had filled a whole tablet—and I went on into the B's. That was the way I started copying what eventually became the entire dictionary. It went a lot faster after so much practice 60 helped me to pick up handwriting speed. Between what I wrote in my tablet, and writing letters, during the rest of my time in prison I would guess I wrote a million words.

I suppose it was inevitable that as my word base broad- 65 ened, I could for the first time pick up a book and read and now begin to understand what the book was saying. Anyone who has read a great deal can imagine the new world that opened. Let me tell you something: from then until I left that 70 prison, in every free moment I had, if I was not reading in the library, I was reading on my bunk. You couldn't have gotten me out of books with a wedge. Between Mr. Muhammad's teachings, my correspondence, my visitors—usually Ella and 75 Reginald—and my reading of books, months passed without my even thinking about being imprisoned. In fact, up to then, I never had been so truly free in my life.

Questions

Question 1: It can be reasonably concluded from the passage that Malcolm X decides to give himself a homemade education because

    A. there's little to do in prison
    B. he has lots of letters to write
    C. he wants to gain and hold people's attention
    D. he wants people to think he's well-educated

Question 2: Which of the following was not an obstacle to Malcolm's self-education?

    A. His handwriting was poor and laborious.
    B. The prison had no supplies for writing.

C. He could only recognize a few words at first.
D. He was amazed to discover how many words there were.

Question 3: When Malcolm describes the dictionary as a "miniature encyclopedia," he means that it

A. contains pictures
B. is organized in alphabetical order
C. is a reference work
D. provides information about society, politics, and history

Question 4: According to the author, the result of Malcolm's education has been to

A. free him from self-imposed limitations
B. free him from the drudgery of prison
C. prepare him for a career when he gets out of prison
D. give him a purpose in life

Question 5: Malcolm's method for study involves these steps:

A. he writes out the meanings of words he doesn't know
B. he copies a page from the dictionary, then reads it aloud
C. he reviews the words with a fellow inmate
D. he moves from topic to topic according to his mood

Question 6: Malcolm's time in prison passed quickly because of

A. Ella and Reginald
B. his correspondence
C. Mr. Muhammad's teaching
D. all of the above

Question 7: Bimbi was an important person in Malcolm's life because

A. Malcolm envied his conversational skill
B. Bimbi shared his dictionary with Malcolm
C. Malcolm wanted to emulate him
D. Bimbi spoke Chinese

Question 8: Malcolm's homemade education began when he

A. understood the need to do legal research
B. became frustrated by his inability to write letters
C. had the opportunity to work in the prison library
D. became embarrassed by not going beyond the eighth grade

Question 9: Malcolm requests a dictionary and tablets to learn new words and to

A. improve his penmanship
B. get a high school diploma
C. read more rapidly
D. see a picture of an aardvark

Question 10: To write in slang bothered Malcolm because

A. he was compared unfavorably to Elijah Muhammad
B. it meant that he wasn't even functional
C. he wanted to be an articulate hustler
D. the shizzle lost its nizzle

Answers

1. C 2. D 3. D 4. A 5. B 6. D 7. C 8. B 9. A 10. B

Commentary

In Question 1, notice how Malcolm refers to his prowess as a street hustler—he remembers how articulate he was and how easily he could "command attention." But he realizes he can't be as effective with street slang in his writing, and now must learn to be articulate in a new way if he still hopes to gain and hold people's attention. In Question 3, you must not be fooled by whatever comparisons you might make between a dictionary and encyclopedia, but instead focus on what Malcolm seems to think is important. In the sentence before Malcolm mentions the term "miniature encyclopedia," he describes how he used the dictionary to learn "about people and places and events from history."

In Question 4, Malcolm's education has no doubt had several benefits, but you must choose the best answer. The fact that Malcolm writes that he had never before been so truly free, while still in prison, indicates that he has overcome his own mental limitations. Questions 2 and 5 simply call for a close, careful reading of the passage.

Once you realize that two of the answer choices are correct, then you know the answer to Question 6 is choice D. Question 7 is trickier because A, B, and C are all true. But the correct answer is C. Bimbi's importance was in that he motivated Malcolm to "emulate" him. If you're observant, you noticed that Question 8 echoes Question 1. Pay attention as you go through the questions and you can save valuable time. The key to Question 9 is understanding why Malcolm would want a tablet. Penmanship is the only logical response (even if you hadn't read the passage). Question 10 is straightforward. A close reading of the text makes answer B the obvious choice.

Passage 6

From What Is Happiness? *by John Ciardi*

The right to pursue happiness is issued to Americans with   1
their birth certificates, but no one seems quite sure which
way it ran. It may be we are issued a hunting license but
offered no game. Jonathan Swift seemed to think so when
he attacked the idea of happiness as "the possession of being
well-deceived," the felicity of being "a fool among knaves."   5
For Swift saw society as Vanity Fair, the land of false goals.

It is, of course, un-American to think in terms of fools and
knaves. We do, however, seem to be dedicated to the idea
of buying our way to happiness. We shall all have made it to
Heaven when we possess enough. And at the same time the   10
forces of American commercialism are hugely dedicated to
making us deliberately unhappy. Advertising is one of our
major industries, and advertising exists not to satisfy desires
but to create them—and to create them faster than any
man's budget can satisfy them. For that matter, our whole   15
economy is based on a dedicated insatiability. We are taught
that to possess is to be happy, and then we are made to
want. We are even told it is our duty to want. It was only a
few years ago, to cite a single example, that car dealers across
the country were flying banners that read "You Auto Buy   20
Now." They were calling upon Americans, as an act
approaching patriotism, to buy at once, with money they did
not have, automobiles they did not really need, and which
they would be required to grow tired of by the time the next
year's models were released.   25

Or look at any of the women's magazines. There, as
Bernard DeVoto once pointed out, advertising begins as
poetry in the front pages and ends as pharmacopoeia and
therapy in the back pages. The poetry of the front matter is
the dream of perfect beauty. This is the baby skin that must   30
be hers. These, the flawless teeth. This, the perfumed breath

she must exhale. This, the sixteen-year-old figure she must display at forty, at fifty, at sixty, and forever.

Once past the vaguely uplifting fiction and feature articles, the reader finds the other face of the dream in the back mat- 35 ter. This is the harness into which Mother must strap herself in order to display that perfect figure. These, the chin straps she must sleep in. This is the salve that restores all, this is her laxative, these are the tablets that melt away fat, these are the hormones of perpetual youth, these are the 40 stockings that hide varicose veins.

Obviously no half-sane person can be completely persuaded either by such poetry or by such pharmacopoeia and orthopedics. Yet someone is obviously trying to buy the dream as offered and spending billions every year in the 45 attempt. Clearly the happiness market is not running out of customers, but what is it trying to buy?

The idea "happiness," to be sure, will not sit still for easy definition: the best one can do is to try to set some extremes to the idea and then work in toward the middle. 50 To think of happiness as acquisitive and competitive will do to set the materialistic extreme. To think of it as the idea one senses in, say, a holy man of India, will do to see the spiritual extreme. That holy man's idea of happiness is in needing nothing from outside himself. In wanting nothing, he lacks 55 nothing. He sits immobile, rapt in contemplation, free even of his own body. Or nearly free of it. If devout admirers bring him food, he eats it; if not, he starves indifferently. Why be concerned? What is physical is an illusion to him. Contemplation is his joy and he achieves it through a fantastically 60 demanding discipline, the accomplishment of which is itself a joy within him.

Is he a happy man? Perhaps his happiness is only another sort of illusion. But who can take it from him? And who will dare say it is more illusory than happiness on the installment 65 plan?

Happiness is never more than partial. There are no pure states of mankind. Whatever else happiness may be, it is neither in having nor in being, but in becoming. What the Founding Fathers declared for us as an inherent right, we should 70 do well to remember, was not happiness but the pursuit of happiness. What they might have underlined, could they have foreseen the happiness market, is the cardinal fact that happiness is in the pursuit itself, in the meaningful pursuit of what is life-engaging and life-revealing, which is to say, in the idea 75 of becoming. A nation is not measured by what it possesses or wants to possess, but by what it wants to become.

By all means let the happiness market sell us minor satisfactions and even minor follies so long as we keep them in scale and buy them out of spiritual change. I am no customer 80 for either puritanism or asceticism. But drop any real spiritual capital at those bazaars and what you come home to will be your own poorhouse.

Questions

Question 1: The author compares the "right to pursue happiness" to

- A. something we can buy
- B. a hunting license
- C. something we can possess
- D. a false goal

Question 2: The author argues that the advertising industry is dedicated to making us unhappy because

- A. happiness is an illusion
- B. we will act more patriotically
- C. happy people don't make the decision to buy things
- D. that will promote a thriving economy

Question 3: Bernard DeVoto is quoted in the passage when he describes advertising as both "poetry" and "pharmacopeia." From the context, you can infer that pharmacopeia means:

A. skin lotions and diet pills
B. illegal drugs
C. false optimism
D. lies and distortion

Question 4: The tone of the passage can best be described as

A. uplifting
B. argumentative
C. sarcastic
D. ironic

Question 5: The author suggests that happiness will be difficult to define. Perhaps the best we can do is

A. define two extremes and work to find a middle ground
B. say what happiness is not
C. look at how other cultures have defined the term
D. rely on a good dictionary

Question 6: For Jonathan Swift, the idea of happiness was all of the following except:

A. the felicity of being
B. a hunting license
C. a fool among knaves
D. the possession of being well-deceived

Question 7: Ciardi suggests that the holy man's idea of happiness may be

A. taking on life-engaging difficulties
B. needing nothing outside oneself
C. happiness on the installment plan
D. possession for its own sake

Question 8: One can conclude that Ciardi believes American commercialism is

A. a creature of both Eastern and Western thought
B. a heightening of our perceptions about life
C. about perfect and therefore static happiness
D. dedicated to making us deliberately unhappy

Question 9: Ciardi suggests that the Founding Fathers viewed happiness in terms of

A. becoming
B. learning
C. possessing
D. discovering

Question 10: The car dealers who advertised "You Auto Buy Now" were hoping

A. that customers would believe in planned obsolescence
B. that customers would believe in rapt contemplation
C. that customers would believe in careful budgeting
D. that customers would believe in the duty to want

Answers

1. B 2. C 3. A 4. D 5. A 6. B 7. B 8. D 9. A 10. D

Commentary

Questions 1 and 5 simply call for close reading. In Question 2, answers C and D are very close and you must decide which is best. Answer D refers to a thriving economy and indeed, the "happiness market" may help support the buying and selling of products and therefore will help stimulate the economy. But this passage operates on a more personal level. The paragraph that contains this section includes several "we, our, and you's." The best answer, C, points to the personal import of what advertisers are trying to do. In Question 3, it may help you to try to recognize at least part of "pharmacopoeia." "Pharma," for example, looks like "pharmacy," a place to buy medicines and other health-related products. The author links poetry to the front pages of a magazine and then points out that pharmacopoeia, found in the back pages, is where readers learn about harnesses, chin straps, salves, laxatives, tablets, hormones, and stockings.

Question 4 refers to the passage as a whole. Because the author is clearly critical of the "happiness market," you can eliminate answer A (uplifting). The passage is not completely straightforward (i.e., answer B, argumentative) because even though the author makes claims—"we are told it is our duty to want," we know that he means the opposite. That makes this passage ironic (D). Sarcasm is a snide, somewhat nasty form of irony and there's no evidence of that here.

Question 6 is fairly straightforward because three of the choices are listed by the reference to Swift. Questions 7, 9, and 10 simply require a close reading of the text. Unfortunately, all four choices might be true responses to Question 8. You must eliminate all but choice D because they are not discussed in the passage. Common sense is not always sufficient.

Social Sciences

Passage 7

"History: Whosestory?" by Ellen Goodman

Certain members of my family—who shall remain name- 1
less—have suggested a bumper sticker for my car: "I Brake
for Antiques." This, of course, is something of an exaggera-
tion. I prefer to think of the afternoons I've spent stopping
along the back roads of New England as adventures in social
history. 5

As I have patiently explained to this same family, what we
call antiques are a record of the real lives that real people
led. They are a kind of down-home proof of the fact that
people beat eggs, drank out of cups, used cupboards.

But what I tend to bring home from my much-maligned 10
jaunts are words. The words of other Americans, captured
in magazines and books. And, occasionally, if I make a hit—
not of the automobile variety—I even get some perspective
on history.

This time, in the musty corner of a store on the old Route 15
1, I found an even mustier, hundred-year-old *Pictorial History
of the United States*. The author of this popular book, one
James D. McCabe, wrote when historians were unencum-
bered by what are now called the "storm troopers of political correctness." 20

So his text brought back a time when even a colorless and
relatively straightforward writer would describe the Amer-

ican past unselfconsciously as "a grand history—a record of the highest achievements of humanity—the noblest, most thrilling and glorious story ever penned on earth." In such star-spangled prose, McCabe called this not only "a Christian nation" but one which was happily "secured for the language and free influences of the all-conquering Anglo-Saxon race."

To read this now, when Christopher Columbus—the man and the day—are being debated, is to see how attitudes and ideas become antique. Speaking in the 1890s, my treasured McCabe did refer to some wrongs the white man inflicted on the natives, but this is not, to put it mildly, *Dances with Wolves*. He tended to regard the "savages" as, uh, fairly uncooperative.

Women show up in this text rarely and African-Americans make cameo appearances as victims of slavery or subjects of policy. And though this author tipped his hat more than once to religious tolerance—coming out squarely against the Salem witch trials—he rather casually referred to Joseph Smith, the leader of the Mormons, as a "cunning imposter."

But what was most striking is what was most typical of my yellowed history. A century ago, the story of America was cast as an onward and upward tale of great men and their institutions and their battles. Our history was one of glory and progress, a parade of Presidents, each of whom came with a fine résumé and nearly all of whom did the right thing.

The text is vastly out-of-date with our sensibilities. We are more contentious now, even about our past. In the schools and colleges, dusty and dry discussions about curricula have turned into heated and highly political debates that were unheard of a hundred years ago. What should be taught and learned about our country? Who has been excluded? What should be included?

They are questions that get to the soul of who we are as a people and what we will think about our country. The debate is often framed now as an attack on the excesses of multiculturalism and increasingly there is an angry edge to it.

The attempt to open up the worldview contained in the 70 writing of men like McCabe is now seen as fragmenting, trivializing, even distorting. Blacks, women, Native Americans, who once criticized history as "his story"—a record of "dead white men"—are now being criticized in turn. 75

I feel no nostalgia in my antique-reading for the comfort and coherence that came from this limited view of the Great Men's March of Time. But what is typical of our present is the difficulty in agreeing on our past, writing an American 80 history. What is typical of our era is the cacophony of voices, once left out, now scrapping for a piece of the historic pie to call their own.

If a historic sense is important, if we define ourselves by 85 our past, then the task now is to find a way to hear the voices of the frontier women, and the Indians at the Little Bighorn, and the people who did not make laws. To include more voices without losing a connecting thread of shared 90 values and ideals that makes us part of something recognizably American.

It's a task that resonates in politics as well as education, in contemporary life as well as history. Can we have diversity 95 and unity in these united states? What antique arguments will cause our descendants to smile smugly when they find them in a country store on a future afternoon?

Questions

Question 1: When the author goes antique hunting, she says she is looking for

A. cups and dishes
B. old furniture

C. attitudes and ideas
D. the contents of cupboards

Question 2: The phrase "star-spangled prose" means

A. stories of American history
B. colorless and straightforward writing
C. unselfconscious writing
D. overly patriotic words

Question 3: All of the following, according to the author, were basically left out of McCabe's *Pictorial History of the United States* except:

A. the Salem witches
B. Native Americans
C. women
D. non-Christians

Question 4: Many people are critical of what they consider a narrow view of history, the so-called record of "dead white men." These people think more diverse viewpoints should be included but others disagree. Those who disagree argue that

A. true Americans are Anglo-Saxon
B. slavery happened a long time ago
C. our presidents mostly did the right thing
D. multiculturalism has gone too far

Question 5: In the last paragraph the author writes "united states" without capital letters. She does so because

A. it was a typographical mistake
B. she wants to emphasize the separate history and
   identity of each state

C. she thinks diversity is more important than unity

D. she is thinking of the country as an antique

Question 6: The author challenges our current notion of political correctness by

A. complimenting our humanitarian achievements

B. reminding us that savages can be fairly uncooperative

C. describing the glory and progress of history

D. asking how future generations will view our prejudices

Question 7: The author's reference to *Dances with Wolves* is

A. a satirical swipe at McCabe's lack of political correctness

B. used in juxtaposition to the victims of slavery

C. an allusion to our thrilling and glorious past

D. a tribute to Kevin Costner's film

Question 8: The author's attitude toward history could be described as

A. smug

B. contentious

C. nostalgic

D. none of the above

Question 9: Traveling the back roads of New England can best be characterized as

A. braking for antiques

B. tipping your hat to tolerance

C. an adventure in social history

D. slicing up the historic pie

Question 10: The author attributes her perspective on history to

A. words
B. tolerance
C. impostors
D. antiques

Answers

1. C 2. D 3. A 4. D 5. B 6. D 7. A 8. D 9. C 10. A

Commentary

Question 1 requires you to compare what the author's family thinks she is looking for when she goes antique shopping and what the author says she is really looking for. Question 2 requires an inference. "Star-spangled" is often associated with patriotism and in this case, the author suggests that writers of a hundred years ago painted a picture of American history without any blemishes. Read carefully for Question 3 and note that although women were rarely mentioned and African-Americans appear only in a few instances, the history writer apparently had quite a bit to say about the Salem witch trials. Question 4 refers to what the author describes as a backlash against political correctness. Answers A, B, and C may fit some of those critics, but D represents the broadest, most inclusive answer.

In Question 5, you can disregard answer A (this text has been proofread several times, believe me) and D (the writer is concerned about current attitudes about who we are as a people). Answer C looks plausible but the author makes it clear in the previous paragraph that while she values hearing many voices, she doesn't want to lose a "connecting thread" (unity). Thus, answer B is the best choice.

Question 6 asks the reader to summarize the author's argument in the essay. A good strategy is to reread the last paragraph to find that summary. If you do, you will find that D is the correct answer. Questions 7, 9, and 10 require nothing more than a close reading of the text. Question 8 is trickier. You can assume that no author would want to be smug or contentious. And although there is some nostalgia in the essay, you would not describe the author's attitude as merely nostalgic. Therefore, the correct answer must be choice D.

Passage 8
The Thin Grey Line by Marya Mannes

"Aw, they all do it," growled the cabdriver. He was talking   1
about cops who took payoffs for winking at double parking,
but his cynicism could as well have been directed at any of
a dozen other instances of corruption, big-time and small-
time. Moreover, the disgust in his voice was overlaid by an   5
unspoken "So what?": the implication that since this was the
way things were, there was nothing anybody could do.

Like millions of his fellow Americans, the cabdriver was
probably a decent human being who had never stolen any-   10
thing, broken any law or willfully injured another; somewhere, a knowledge of what was probably right had kept him
from committing what was clearly wrong. But that knowledge had not kept a thin grey line that separates the two   15
conditions from being daily greyer and thinner—to the point
that it was hardly noticeable.

On one side of this line are They: the bribers, the cheaters,
the chiselers, the swindlers, the extortioners. On the other   20
side are We—both partners and victims. They and We are
now so perilously close that the only mark distinguishing us
is that They get caught and We don't.

The same citizen who voices his outrage at police cor-   25
ruption will slip the traffic cop on his block a handsome
Christmas present in the belief that his car, nestled under a
"No Parking" sign, will not be ticketed. The son of that nice
woman next door has a habit of stealing cash from her   30
purse because his allowance is smaller than his buddies'. Your

son's friend admitted cheating at exams because "everybody does it."

Bit by bit, the resistance to and immunity against wrong that a healthy social body builds up by law and ethics and the dictation of conscience have broken down. And instead of the fighting indignation of a people outraged by those who prey on them, we have the admission of impotence: "They all do it."

Now, failure to uphold the law is no less corrupt than violations of the law. And the continuing shame of this country now is the growing number of Americans who fail to uphold and assist enforcement of the law, simply—and ignominiously—out of fear. Fear of "involvement," fear of reprisal, fear of "trouble." A man is beaten by hoodlums in plain daylight and in view of bystanders. These people not only fail to help the victim, but like the hoodlums, flee before the police can question them. A city official knows of a colleague's bribe but does not report it. A pedestrian watches a car hit a woman but leaves the scene, to avoid giving testimony. It happens every day. And if the police get cynical at this irresponsibility, they are hardly to blame. Morale is a matter of giving support and having faith in one another; where both are lacking, "law" has become a worthless word.

How did we get this way? What started this blurring of what was once a thick black line between the lawful and the lawless? What makes a "regular guy," a decent fellow, accept a bribe? What makes a nice kid from a middle-class family take money for doing something he must know is not only illegal but wrong?

When you look into the background of an erring "kid" you will often find a comfortable home and a mother who will tell you, with tears in her eyes, that she "gave him everything." She probably did, to his everlasting damage. Fearing her son's disapproval, the indulgent mother denies him nothing except responsibility. Instead of growing up, he grows to believe that the world owes him everything.

Today, no one has to take any responsibility. The psychiatrists, the sociologists, the novelists, the playwrights have gone a long way to help promote irresponsibility. Nobody really is to blame for what he does. It's Society. It's Environment. It's a Broken Home. It's an Underprivileged Area. But it's hardly ever You.

Now we find a truckload of excuses to absolve the individual from responsibility for his actions. A fellow commits a crime because he's basically insecure, because he hated his stepmother at nine, or because his sister needs an operation. A policeman loots a store because his salary is too low. A city official accepts a payoff because it's offered to him. Members of minority groups, racial or otherwise, commit crimes because they can't get a job, or are unacceptable to the people living around them. The words "right" and "wrong" are foreign to these people.

But honesty is the best policy. Says who? Anyone willing to get laughed at. But the laugh is no laughing matter. It concerns the health and future of a nation. It involves the two-dollar illegal bettor as well as the corporation price-fixer, the college-examination cheater and the payroll-padding Congressman, the expense-account chiseler, the seller of pornography and his schoolboy reader, the bribed judge and the stealing delinquent. All these people may represent a minority. But when, as it appears now, the majority excuse themselves from responsibility by accepting corruption as natural to society ("They all do it"), this society is bordering on total confusion. If the line between right and wrong is finally erased, there is no defense against the power of evil.

Before this happens—and it is by no means far away—it might be well for the schools of the nation to substitute for the much-argued issue of prayer a daily lesson in ethics, law,

and responsibility to society that would strengthen the conscience as exercise strengthens muscles. And it would be 115
even better if parents were forced to attend it. For corruption is not something you read about in the papers and leave
to courts. We are all involved.

Questions

Question 1: The author's "thin grey line" refers to an imagi-
nary difference between all of the following except:

A. bribery and extortion
B. right and wrong
C. conscience and dishonesty
D. lawful and lawless

Question 2: A witness who leaves the scene of an accident
without giving a report is cited as an example of

A. forgetfulness
B. a failure to uphold the law
C. weakness
D. cowardice

Question 3: The author argues that a once thick black line is
blurring because of

A. permissive parenting
B. social change
C. bad role models
D. too much prosperity

Question 4: The cabdriver who growls at cops who take
bribes—"Aw, they all do it," he says—is describing a serious social problem. The solution, according to the author is

A. better law enforcement
B. less political corruption
C. better civic education
D. for each person to accept responsibility

Question 5: "Morale" in the context of the passage (line 56) means

A. pride
B. encouragement and trust
C. a spirit of teamwork
D. a strong work ethic

Question 6: The nice kid's father crosses the thin grey line by

A. an admission of impotence
B. arguing in favor of school prayer
C. padding his income tax returns
D. swindling criminals to balance the scales

Question 7: Americans who fail to uphold the law suffer from

A. a fear of involvement
B. a fear of reprisal
C. a fear of "trouble"
D. all of the above

Question 8: The author argues that if the line between right and wrong is erased, the consequences will be

A. defenselessness against the power of evil
B. the rise of the corporation price-fixer
C. that nobody will really be to blame
D. that society will border on total confusion

Question 9: When the author uses the phrase "honesty is the best policy," she is being

    A. hopeful
    B. ironic
    C. prescriptive
    D. patriotic

Question 10: According to the author, indulgent mothers deny their children

    A. heroes
    B. opportunity
    C. excuses
    D. responsibility

Answers

    1. A 2. B 3. A 4. D 5. B 6. C 7. D 8. A 9. B 10. D

Commentary

In Question 1 you need to recognize that "bribers" and "extortioners" are both listed as being on the same side of the grey line. Turn "bribers" and "extortioners" into "bribery" and "extortion," and voila—you've got your answer. Question 2 can be answered by looking back a few sentences to the beginning of the paragraph—everything that follows is an example of "failure to uphold the law." Question 3 requires you to group a variety of examples of how mothers and fathers baby their children or take illegal short cuts as "permissive parenting." The answer to Question 4 asks you to look from the very beginning of the passage (the cab driver) to the very end where the author makes her point. But you also have to reverse the statement. The author says, "No one has to take any responsibility." By inference, we can conclude that she means "everyone must take responsibility." For Question 5, replace these words in the passage, "a matter of giving support" with this part of the answer—"encouragement"—and "having faith in one another" with "trust."

Questions 6, 7, and 10 simply require a careful reading of the passage. Question 8 is more difficult because choices A and D are both true. Choice A is correct, though, because it's a "consequence" of the "total confusion" mentioned in choice D. Question 9 demands an understanding of the tone of the entire passage. You should consider "irony" as a distinct possibility whenever it appears as an answer choice. Authors often use irony to make a point. Remember that.

Credits

About the Authors

Randall McCutcheon, nationally recognized by the U.S. Department of Education for innovation in curriculum, has authored eight books, including *Can You Find It?*, a guide to teaching research skills to high school students, which received the 1990 Ben Franklin Award for best self-help book of the year; *Get Off My Brain*, a survival guide for students who hate to study, which was selected by the New York Public Library as one of 1998's Best Books for Teenagers; and three textbooks for speech and journalism courses.

After nearly a decade working in radio and television, McCutcheon taught for twenty-seven years in both public and private schools in Iowa, Massachusetts, Nebraska, and New Mexico. He was selected the State Teacher of the Year in Nebraska in 1985, and in 1987 he was named the National Forensic League National Coach of the Year. Elected to the N.F.L. Hall of Fame in 2001, he concluded a successful career as a high school speech coach. In twenty-seven years, his speech teams won twenty-five state and five national championships.

James Schaffer is the chair of the English Department at Nebraska Wesleyan University where he teaches writing and journalism courses. He has a Ph.D. in English from the University of Virginia and has been frequently involved in developing writing curricula, assisting with a freshman writing program, and leading writing workshops. He is the author of three textbooks and numerous articles.

Schaffer was a finalist for the Teacher-in-Space program in 1985 and, as a result, became a speaker and presenter for NASA. He has given more than four hundred programs on the space shuttle to professional organizations, community groups, and schools. He was named Nebraska's Aerospace Educator of the Year.

As a journalism advisor, he has lead his publication's staffs to numerous state and national awards, including the Best Magazine of the Year award from the Columbia Scholastic Press Association. Schaffer and his wife, Mary Lynn, also an educator, have three children—Suzanne, Sarah, and Stephen.